*As Chance
would have it*

As Chance would have it

A Study in Coincidences

HANS C. MOOLENBURGH, MD

Index compiled by Mary Kirkness

SAFFRON WALDEN
THE C.W. DANIEL COMPANY LIMITED

First published in Great Britain in 1998
by The C. W. Daniel Company Limited
1 Church Path, Saffron Walden,
Essex, CB10 1JP, United Kingdom

© Hans C. Moolenburgh, MD, 1998

ISBN 0 85207 317 8

Produced in association with Book Production Consultants plc
25–27 High Street, Chesterton, Cambridge, CB4 1ND, UK
Designed & typeset by Ward Partnership, Saffron Walden, Essex
Printed in England by Hillman Printers (Frome) Ltd, England

Contents

ACKNOWLEDGEMENT

I am grateful to my wife An for having read the whole manuscript, giving sound advice and fishing out the most glaring mistakes.

DEDICATION

This book is dedicated to my VITIS friends.
Their enthusiastic acclaim of my lecture on coincidences
gave me the impulse to write this book.

WHAT IS COINCIDENCE?

That is the question I am going to analyse and answer in this book. I first became interested in the subject in 1960 when a booklet was published in Holland with the title (translated) *The role played by coincidence and fate in our daily life*. It had originally been written in German. The writer was Wilhelm Scholz and one of the stories in that book stayed in my memory. From time to time I told it to patients during office hours to teach them that there exists a certain mysterious pattern in life and that things do not just happen at random.

Here is how I remembered the story:

A young couple, newly engaged to be married, is going for a walk in a deep and silent wood. Somewhere they find a secluded corner where the undergrowth is soft with green moss and here they have a lovely and thoroughly satisfying time together.

When they walk home the young woman suddenly exclaims in dismay "My engagement ring!". That new and beautiful ring has slipped from her finger somewhere and is gone. Retracing their steps, they look for the place where they have been lying on the moss, but they cannot find the ring. Either they are in the wrong spot or the ring has tumbled into some hole.

A year later as a newly-wed couple, with a new ring for her, of course, bride and bridegroom return to that wood with its bittersweet memories. They wander around and at a certain moment they reach a secluded spot and lo and behold, a beautiful ox eye daisy has sprung up and in the middle of the flower the long-lost engagement ring lies waiting for the astonished bride.

In December 1996, after having told this story from time to time for many years, I had to give a lecture on coincidence to my Dutch-Flemish medical doctors' group and of course I decided to start my talk with the story of the ring. While I was mulling over my lecture it suddenly struck me that there was an inconsistency in the story. How could an unfolding flower keep an engagement ring, which it must have pushed up from the ground, in its heart? It was strange never to have thought about it before, but there it was, staring me in the face.

So I hunted through my catalogue and located the book, which I had not seen for 36 years. I looked up the story and there it was, but not quite as I had thought. Apparently my memory had played me false. Here is the real story:

There was a painter called Moritz von Schwind, who was painting frescos for the Wartburg, a famous castle in what was formerly East

Germany. He stayed with his wife in a nearby hotel. One day they went for a walk in the beautiful Anna Valley and while they were walking and talking she gathered some wild flowers. Suddenly she discovered that she had lost her engagement ring. They searched for it for a long time but they could not find it.

One year later Mr and Mrs von Schwind (the name means "that which vanishes") were revisiting the Anna Valley and Mrs von Schwind reminded her husband of how she had lost her engagement ring just about here. At that very moment they noticed a splendid yellow mullein and at the top of it there was the engagement ring, neatly pierced by the arrow-like flower (in Holland we call it a "torch").

I now understood that the inconsistency in the story was due to my own imagination. This flower could easily have pushed through the ring, carrying it upwards as it grew.

Von Schwind was a painter of fairy-tales and Wilhelm Scholz ends his story by stating that nature had momentarily borrowed the character of a fairy-tale to be in tune with this painter.

The change I brought to this story does not reflect very favourably on yours truly, but does show what time can do to a memory. Happily, in the stories that follow such distortion has not taken place. From 1969 I have kept a diary and when a coincidence happens I write it down straightaway, just as it was. I also kept a diary during the Second World War and one of the stories is derived from that source. So you can rest assured that all the stories you read really happened as I describe them. They have not been altered by my imagination.

There were two ways to go about the writing of this book. The first one was to assemble stories right and left, as I did in my *Meetings with Angels*. The other way was to keep it personal and only tell stories about my own experiences. This of course makes the book rather autobiographical and thus less interesting. Yet I chose the latter way, not out of vanity, but for another reason. Coincidences happen in everyone's lives, but usually they are quickly forgotten. That is a pity, for they are really quite interesting.

By writing down coincidences in my own life, you have the guarantee that they happened just as I describe them. Moreover, and this is at least as important, you have stories from someone just like you: a normal average person. This will make it easier for you to exclaim time and again, "But a similar thing happened to me!"

When that happens you have made me a happy man for then I have made you alert to that mysterious phenomenon we call coincidence, which adds flavour to our lives and makes living more fun.

In Dutch the word for coincidence is "toeval":

toe = towards
val = to fall.

In German it is "zufall", with exactly the same meaning.

Something falls towards you out of the blue.

So let us start with those coincidences in my life that have to do with encounters. This will give the reader an idea of what it is all about.

Sometimes I will have to describe a situation before I can go on to the coincidence connected with it, otherwise the coincidence cannot be savoured to the full and that is what must be done with these stories. They must be sampled like wine.

May many happy coincidences abound in your life, as they have done in mine.

IN THE CENTRE of my home town of Haarlem there is a big, modern chemist's shop, full of polished, shining counters, endless rows of bottles and white-coated girls dispensing to suffering humanity the potent drugs without which 20th-century man cannot be happy.

20 years ago, in the midst of this excess of competent pharmacists and assistants, there used to move an elderly, slightly crippled fat man, who slowly, like an old and tired dog, puffed his way from one client to the other. It was as if someone had forgotten to remove an ancient piece of furniture and now everyone had become so accustomed to it that it stayed on, while all that business-like competency swirled around him. It was an anachronism if ever there was one.

This man played a very important part in that pharmacy, outdated as he was.

Those who have lived in a village or a small town remember a shop, be it a bakery, a greengrocer's or a butcher's, where people not only came to buy, but also to chat, to socialize, to exchange the latest news. The centre of all this activity was the owner of the shop, man or woman, who was shopkeeper, social worker, host or hostess and comforter rolled into one.

Such a man was this old assistant, going about his quite old-fashioned way, loved by all and sundry and – without anyone realising it – being far more the face of the chemist's shop than the pharmacist himself, who was usually enthroned in a secluded glass case all by himself somewhere at the back of the shop.

There was in the life of this old, fat man one overwhelming sorrow: the decline of his beloved Roman Catholic Church. So what he did was to buy up as much of the interiors of discarded churches as his purse could stand and his flat could accommodate. Thus, while several churches were demolished or converted to suit one of the many requirements of modern bureaucracy, his flat filled to overflowing with statues, of Mary and the Saints, crosses, candelabras, priests' robes, and even, in one room, a whole altar. A Catholic church reduced to the size of a four-room flat. I was his doctor and when I first entered his flat, the feeling of anachronism he always gave me deepened into bewilderment and even disorientation as he proudly showed me his rooms crammed full of sacred objects.

At home also the old fat man was a blessing for many. Youngsters abandoned by their parents were taken under his wing and led into a meaningful and useful life.

The highlight of the year for this old man was the visit to Rome at Easter. Though walking became more and more of a problem as he grew older, and while he resolutely refused to have his arthritic hips

I

Encounters
and
coincidences

operated on, which back then was still considered a major operation, he never missed Rome and that supreme moment when the Pope appeared on the balcony, saying the Urbe et Orbi.

One day this old and dear patient of mine was again in Rome for the great occasion. Slowly he moved through the milling crowd of pilgrims, thousands of them, out of breath and over-heated and trying to find a spot from where he could see the Pope.

At last he stopped to give his painful hips a rest. A man standing next to him gave him a compassionate glance and said, "You are surely a Dutchman."

"Yes, I am," admitted my patient.

"What is the matter with your legs?"

"Arthritis of the hips. It causes me a considerable amount of pain and walking is difficult."

"You know," the man said confidentially to my patient, "if I were you I should go to a doctor in Haarlem. His name is Moolenburgh and perhaps he can help you."

Well, of course I couldn't and I hadn't and apparently my fame was greater than my actual capacity for curing, but just imagine in your mind's eye this situation. The crowd of thousands of pilgrims, comprising all nationalities, and this patient of mine being recommended his own doctor by a totally unknown man standing next to him. That is what I mean by coincidence.

Coincidence means that two (or more) different events are happening at the same time. Looking at them in a superficial way they are not related to each other and yet they form a new and rather mysterious whole. In a flash a pattern emerges that usually remains under the surface of our existence and yet is always present, waiting for the right circumstances to expose itself.

The above case was of course rather spectacular, it could hardly be missed, and my patient told me about it as soon as he was home. Sometimes however a coincidence occurs in such a low-key way that one easily shrugs it off as just one of those things.

On 24 February 1993 my youngest son graduated in communication sciences at the University of Amsterdam.

The festivities were going to take place in one of the university buildings and my wife and I decided to take the train rather than running the risk of a traffic jam and arriving too late.

We alighted at the Central Station in Amsterdam with about a thousand commuters streaming into the city and hundreds of people leaving the city. We moved slowly towards the exit in this human whirlpool, when suddenly we heard an exclamation and there was our youngest son. We had not expected him there and he had not expected us either. What he was doing at the station, although he lived in Amsterdam, I do not know, but we were very lucky to have met him, because we then heard that the graduation was going to take place in a different building from the one originally planned. Our son was not aware of the fact that we were ignorant of this change of plans, and the risk of missing the ceremony, had we not heard from him where to find this other building, was very great indeed. The original building and this other one were quite a distance apart.

Here we see another aspect of coincidence. It sometimes goes out of its way to help you, giving you the right push at the right time. It is as if the phenomenon *likes* to help us from time to time. At the end of this book I will try to make some sense of these occurrences, but for the time being I only want to register what happened.

The next story is part of a much larger one so, in order to make the point clear, I have to dive into the larger story for some pages.

After the war the Dutch Police were in rather a mess. In a special camp (Schalkhaar), the Nazis had trained policemen according to Nazi standards and these SS-like policemen permeated the police force. A major clean-up operation was called for and my father, up until then a well-known Public Prosecutor in Amsterdam, was appointed Director General of the Dutch state police with the special task of finding the Schalkharen men and throwing them out and, in general, eradicating all Nazi influence.

Right at the start he received a request from General Eisenhower and Field-Marshal Montgomery that if he ever found proof of betrayal concerning the battle of Arnhem, he should tell them as soon as possible.

In 1946 he received a telephone call from Monsieur Boursicot, Director General of the French state police. He told my father that a high-up German officer had been caught in France and that papers had been found on this man, proving that the battle of Arnhem, in military circles known as Operation Market Garden, had been lost because of betrayal by a Dutch double agent.

Father asked Boursicot to send him this German officer straight away but Boursicot told him that the man was suspected of war crimes and had to stand trial in France. As a matter of fact he literally said, "No, we are going to shoot him here." He would, however, send father the papers and indeed they arrived the next day by special messenger at Amsterdam Airport. Father read these papers and

7

discovered from them that a Dutch double agent called Lindemans, but known by his code name King Kong (because of his enormous strength), had early in September 1944 heard in the headquarters of Prince Bernhard in Belgium that great airborne landings were expected along the Wijk bij Duurstede-Appeldoorn line (the Prince was not personally involved in it). He hastily went through the German lines and told this story to staff at the German Headquarters in the Netherlands and they concluded rightly that the real target was the bridge at Arnhem.

Father straightaway took these papers to his immediate boss, the Minister of Justice, and this man, on reading them said, "Good Lord, this is highly compromising for the Prince."

"Maybe," my father answered, "but I have promised Eisenhower and Montgomery that if I ever discovered treason in the battle of Arnhem, I would directly inform them."

"Where is this King Kong?" asked the Minister.

"We have him in prison in Scheveningen. He has already been unmasked as a double agent, though this part of his treason is new."

"What are you going to do about it?"

"The day after tomorrow I will personally interrogate him."

The Minister put the papers in a drawer of his desk where they vanished from sight and father never talked to King Kong for the next day he was found dead in his cell. The official verdict was "suicide". Not so long afterwards a great intrigue was got up against my father and he was relieved of his position with an impressive medal and maintenance of his salary to sweeten the pill. When the Minister of Justice asked him which function he would like for the rest of his professional career, Father answered, "A position where I will never have anything to do with a Minister of Justice or a Secretary of State." So he became a judge in Amsterdam and enjoyed himself immensely. In 1966 he died and I always regretted that the King Kong story died with him.

Fourteen years after his death I wrote a book about a colleague of mine. He had been put on trial because he had healed a child with cancer using unorthodox methods. The book was called *Science Knows No Tears* and in it I used the King Kong story. I wanted to demonstrate the fact that, at every moment in life, decisions are taken which can determine the course of history, however small they look at that moment. I asked myself what happened to the other possibilities that were discarded at the moment of decision. Did they just vanish into thin air, or are there parallel universes where these other possibilities are worked out?

Then I used the King Kong story in veiled terms as an illustration. I wrote: "In 1946 there was a high official in the Hague. Let us call him Mr A. One day he received a telephone call from his French colleague Mr B."

I then proceeded to describe the exact sequence of events you have just read. I ended the passage with: "Many years after the incriminating papers vanished, the moving film "A Bridge Too Far" began its triumphal journey round the world. It was one of the most brilliant pieces of disinformation – be it unconscious on the part of the maker – I had ever seen and it seemed strange that, through a freak of fate, I was one of the very few people who knew what really happened, because Mr A had told me the story himself."

In 1983 I received a telephone call from a Mr Tiemens who asked me, "Doctor, the story about Mr A and Mr B in your book *Science Knows No Tears*: was it just fiction or is it a signal?"

This was what I had secretly been hoping for.

"It is a signal," I said.

He jumped in his car and straightaway drove the more than 100 kilometres to my place. He lived in Arnhem at the time.

When he came to my house, he told me that for years on end, as a military man, he had been interested in the battle of Arnhem. He was even engaged in writing a book about the subject but still some information was missing.

When I told him who Mr A and Mr B were he said, "This is the missing link. Now I can finish my book. It is the keystone of the whole story."

He even went to Boursicot, who was still alive but not much use to him, as the good man had grown rather woolly-minded.

When Tiemens had finished his book (*Aspects of the Battle of Arnhem*) he invited me for the festive launch of his book in Schaarsbergen in a restaurant opposite the bunker where, during the battle of Arnhem, the Germans coordinated their air defence. The date this was going to happen was 25 April 1984.

The reader absolutely has to know all these facts in order to appreciate the events that followed for at this moment coincidence stepped in.

First one should know that my brother studied medicine in Leiden and he had a close friend called William. This William was a very handsome man, a sort of Greek God come alive, while neither my brother nor myself will ever win a beauty contest. The two friends were commonly called "the Beauty and the Beast". The Beauty later on became a well-known specialist in Haarlem, and I regularly referred patients to him though we never visited each other's houses.

So I was rather surprised when, on 18 April 1984 at 6 o'clock in the afternoon, just after I had finished work, this William walked in and sat down for a casual chat. He did not have any special reason for this visit, it was just friendly small talk. This of course was slightly peculiar, after we had lived half a kilometre away from each other for 30 years. In hindsight, I believe I can rationalise his visit. It was not so long before his sudden death and I rather think that, subconsciously, he felt it coming and was suddenly overwhelmed by nostalgia for his student days and was using me as a substitute for my brother, who did not live close by.

Anyhow we talked for three-quarters of an hour and in the course of the conversation I told him about Tiemens and his book and the King Kong story.

"What!" he exclaimed. "My wife should know about this as soon as possible. Her whole resistance group was betrayed by King Kong and though she herself escaped, she lost several friends. Wouldn't it be possible for her to go to Schaarsbergen, too, when the book is launched?"

I said I would call Tiemens, who gracefully invited the Beauty and his wife. Tiemens is a very nice man.

Accompanied by our wives, William and I went to Schaarsbergen, where we were presented with copies of the book, and went home, but there it did not stop.

When William's wife read Tiemens' book she became very excited. Tiemens had suggested that perhaps King Kong was not in his grave, and she began to pull a lot of strings to get the grave opened. The King Kong affair burst into the daily paper and became a big issue. At last the body of King Kong was dug up and it was indeed he who was lying in that grave. They put him to rest again but I doubt if it was in peace. However, first they did an autopsy and found a lot of arsenic in his body that should not have been there. Nothing was done about it, though.

To conclude this story: in 1992 another book was published, called *Spy in the Garden* (I have translated the title) by Bob de Graaff, and there to my great delight I read that the papers sent by Boursicot to my father had at last been discovered somewhere in a forgotten desk in the Ministry of Justice. They confirmed the story my father had told. Bob came to the conclusion that perhaps the battle around Arnhem itself was not influenced so much by King Kong's betrayal, but as a direct consequence of the information he had given the

German High Command, they had strengthened their positions at Nijmegen and this had led to the Allied armies being held up for so long that they could not bring the necessary reinforcements to the encircled troops in Arnhem. So the catastrophe of Market Garden was, after all, partly due to King Kong's treason.

May I summarize this story to put the coincidence in perspective? I had been a medical doctor for 31 years in Haarlem, William had been in Haarlem as a medical specialist for at least as many years. On 18 April 1984 he paid me for the first time a social call, on impulse, and received information from me about Tiemens' book and about the King Kong treason. This set in train a whole avalanche of events which eventually led to King Kong being exhumed and the whole King Kong story hitting the Dutch press in a big way. I believe that the King Kong story having become a hot item impelled Bob de Graaff to do his research and this brought to light the document sent from France to my father in 1946, proving King Kong's treason. William was a king-pin in the whole series of events but a completely accidental one.

Murder will out, it is said, and Lindemans' treason led to a great slaughter.

This story shows us another aspect of the mysterious way in which coincidence works. In this case it helped to bring many relevant facts about the battle of Arnhem to light which otherwise would have been buried for ever. Apparently coincidence loves the truth.

The next story is another example of how the phenomenon of coincidence can make life easier.

During the war there lived in Haarlem a watchmaker with his two spinster daughters Corrie and Betsy. They lived in a typically old Dutch house, very narrow and 4 storeys high, a little bit lopsided, in a street full of shops called Barteljorisstraat. A Barteljoris was an officer of law enforcement 400 years ago. The street came out upon the market square with its beautiful old cathedral. In this church there is a famous organ upon which Mozart has played.

The family I am talking about was called ten Boom and they were devout Christians. During the war they began to hide Jews from the Germans and they saved many of them from the Holocaust. In the end they were betrayed. The 80-year-old father died in captivity some weeks after his arrest, the daughter Betsy died completely emaciated in the concentration camp, Ravensbrück, and a brother who had also been arrested died soon after the war from illness. 100,000 women died in Ravensbrück but Corrie ten Boom was released, probably as the result of an administrative error, during the same week in which all the women in her barrack were murdered. Corrie became a world-famous evangelist, visiting 64 countries and daring to visit places where no one else could go. In the seventies I became her physician and she told me that there was a great desire in her heart. She wanted her old home in the Barteljorisstraat, usually called the Béjé, where so many Jews had been saved, to become a centre of remembrance and a place of evangelisation. Sadly, the house had in the meantime passed into the possession of another watchmaker and he did not want to sell it for that purpose. So "Aunt Corrie", as everyone called her, died (on her 91st birthday, 15 April 1983) before her wish could be fulfilled. On 17 April 1986, I had an unexpected visit from an American evangelist called Mike Evans. He told me the astonishing news that, on the spur of the moment (or, as he said, because the Lord had told him to do it) he had flown to Holland and bought the Béjé. He now wanted to make it into a place of remembrance but not knowing the Dutch situation and having heard that I knew Aunt Corrie well, he needed my help. This was a difficult question but just that week I had met one of my former patients while out on my daily walk. He was a newly-retired manager of a small bank in Haarlem and he had told me that time was weighing heavily on his hands, so it seemed to me a good idea to ask this man, who was bored to distraction, if he might try to organise the ten Boom museum.

Against the urgings of my assistant, Emily, who did not think much of my choice, I asked him to organise the whole project and I must say that he did a splendid job. Within a year the house had been restored exactly as it had been during the war, furniture and all, and he had even persuaded a watchmaker to take the ground floor as his workshop. High up in the house could still be seen the ingenious hiding-place behind the wall in what had once been Aunt Corrie's bedroom, where several Jews had evaded arrest, when the final raid on the house by the Nazis came in 1944.

As Aunt Corrie's lifestory had been published in the USA in *The Hiding Place* and a film with the same name (partly filmed in Haarlem) had been shown all over the States, soon after the official opening of the house whole droves of Americans, thousands of them, came to visit the new Museum and the house became a sort of Christian counterpart to the Ann Frank House in Amsterdam. The success exceeded our wildest expectations.

I do not know if the results of all his work went to the head of the retired banker who in the meantime had become the manager of the Béjé but it is sad to say that now and then he used some of the money from the donations box (we did not charge for admission to the museum, it was all on a voluntary basis) for slightly different purposes from those they were meant for. In the end this meant that the manager had to leave the Béjé. Of course I had kept an exact record of all his valiant deeds and his less valiant dippings. All that time I had been a member of the Advisory Board. Soon after my involvement with the museum came to an end.

In 1996 I decided that my life had been interesting enough to write my memoirs, not for publication but for those of my descendants in the 21st century who might want to know how we lived in that great age of revolution, the 20th century.

In the first week of November 1996 I had arrived at the tragi-comic episode of the Béjé, the adventures of the manager and his donations box and my grudging admittance to my assistant that once again she had been right in her assessment of someone whom I had trusted completely and whom she had mistrusted from the beginning.

I needed the file on this man for my memoirs, so I asked Emily to find it in the attic and put it on my desk, which she did straight-away. So there it was, waiting to be included in my eventful life-story.

Hardly had the file been placed on my desk when I received a telephone call from a very important lady in Haarlem. She was one of those busy people who serve on all sorts of committees and she was involved in various cultural events. She wanted to have an urgent talk with me so, late in the afternoon on 6 November, there she was, charming as ever and radiating an air of being in the midst of all things important. A little bit like Rabbit in Winnie-the-Pooh. I nearly felt important myself.

She told me that a certain man had asked to become involved in a certain cultural project in the town. It was rather an extensive organization with quite a lot of money. She wanted to know if this man was the right person for the job.

When I asked for his name, she said it was the same man who had years ago been manager of the ten Boom museum.

With a nonchalant gesture, as if I were taking a white rabbit out of a top hat, I picked up the file from my desk and said, "Of course, let us have a look. I have to refresh my memory for a moment." He did not get the job.

So that is what I mean. I had not seen her since 15 April 1988, the official opening of the Béjé, and now on 8 November 1996. 8½ years later, she suddenly calls on me for advice about a man whose file was lying on my desk that very day.

The phenomenon of coincidences can save you a lot of valuable time.

This time-saving element was also conspicuous in the next episode. In 1992 I was on holiday in Southern France near Montauroux in the Var district. Even there it can rain cats and dogs in the summer as it did on 24 June.

AS CHANCE
WOULD HAVE IT

"Let's go to the coast," I said to my wife. "Perhaps it is better there."

So we drove over the beautiful red Estorel mountain range towards Théoule on the Mediterranean coast. While we were driving south I said, "My friend John W. lives somewhere in these parts."

John was a chap I knew from my student days. We were members of the same student corps and even the same club. Every new year, when the new members arrive, about 25 men form what is called a club. In a year when 200 students become a member, about 8 clubs are formed and some stay intact for a lifetime.

"I have no idea how we could find his address for I do not even know in which town or village he lives," I continued. "How stupid of me not to have looked up his address in Holland."

When we reached the coast the rain stopped and the clouds began to break. We walked the wet streets of Théoule and came to a small picturesque harbour. There were not many people about, only one elderly lady walking with a small child, apparently her grandchild. We stood still and I said something nice about the little girl in what I thought was impeccable French.

The lady looked at me with something like compassion and said in my native tongue, "You're Dutch of course."

I had to confess that this indeed was the case and hoped that she had deduced this from my considerable height. We exchanged some small talk and went on our way, but suddenly my wife said to me, "Wait, perhaps she knows John's address." She went back to the lady with the grandchild and asked, "It's a strange question but do you happen to know a John W.?"

"But of course," she said. "He and his wife are among our best friends. He lives in Grasse."

There and then she gave us his address and telephone number.

We visited my friend that week and had an excellent dinner at his flat overlooking the bay at Cannes.

Once more I wondered how great the odds were against us meeting just that one Dutchwoman in a place at least 25 miles from Grasse (and even more from the place where we stayed during our holiday) who could give us John's address and telephone number. I am not a mathematician but they must be enormous.

I hope that by now I have made the point clear that there is more to coincidence than meets the eye. Of course there are always people who will say, "So what?". That cannot he helped.

Nicoll, in his *Commentaries on the Teaching of Gurdieff & Ouspensky*, says that there are two sorts of people: those who have a "magnetic centre" and those who have no magnetic centre. What is this centre? It is not easy to define. Materialistic science has got everything cut and dried and thrown mystery onto the dungheap. Everything is described in scientific terms. Essentially, all data are derived from sensory perception and our world is explained in terms of itself. That somewhere mystery pervades all existence and that many things cannot be explained and probably never will be explained irritates the materialistic scientist like a wasp sting. Somehow he lacks the capacity to detect mystery and to recognize phenomena that, though happening in this world, do not belong to it but to some other, probably higher, dimension. It is that dimension which provides life with meaning. A feeling for mystery comes from a magnetic centre and mystery is a dirty word in our universities.

In our materialistic age, the magnetic centre has atrophied nearly completely in leading scientific circles, and this leaves its mark on our whole educational system. That is why so many people nowadays suffer from a feeling of meaninglessness. It has become a ubiquitous disease, which young people especially try to heal with drugs. These, in the end, make the feeling only worse. Another way to escape this feeling is by trying to increase the amount of decibels, numbing the intolerable awareness of nothingness.

Young people acting like this are not the worst part of society. They long for a glimpse of the mystery, thus showing that part of their magnetic centre is still active.

About the stories I have told thus far, someone without a magnetic centre will say, "We have not found the explanation yet but no doubt when we have more information it will be found some day. Wait till we get to work with our new generation of computers. It is all a question of statistical calculation of probabilities. The stories you have told are not convincing at all and they should be called what they are: just mere coincidences."

Someone with a magnetic centre, on the other hand, will recognise the mystery, will feel attracted to that mystery, and will remember examples of it in his or her own life, becoming more alert to them when they happen in future.

For this is a fact that has been noticed by those who are on the look-out for coincidences: as soon as they adopt an expectant attitude, coincidences begin to multiply and reveal a breathtaking pattern beneath the apparently random nature of existence. Apart from the awe that inspires in those who experience this, it is quite fun when it happens. Life begins to sparkle and the dull clouds of materialism are blown away.

MANY COINCIDENCES ARE connected with our bodies.

At the time of Descartes we acquired a nasty habit. We have learned to consider the body as merely physical and the spirit as quite separate from the body and purely spiritual. The unity has been lost and this has caused a split in our way of thinking with grave consequences. Our whole civilisation has taken on a schizophrenic character.

Thoughts often contain no wisdom, as can be seen in the teachings of many modern philosophers, though thoughts definitely are spiritual, but the body, though "merely" physical is wise beyond comparison. It knows exactly how to repair the most difficult lesions, how to monitor the most delicate and intricate processes and how to survive in nearly impossible circumstances.

The immune system, for instance, is so complicated that we understand only a fraction of it. Take as an example the fight against cancer. When a cancer cell develops, a certain white blood cell comes along, and, just like a bullfighter in Spain with the bull in the arena, plants something on that cell which can be compared to a little white flag. Along comes a killer cell, it sees the little white flag and eats the cancer cell. Some cancer cells however are smart and place a little hood over the flag, and thus escape detection. The immune system has found ways to discover that hood and so on.

Compare these wise processes with the really stupid systems scientists have believed in all through history and one sees that our spirit has not even got a ten-thousandth part of the wisdom of our bodies and that our bodies in essence are very spiritual.

As an example of the systems scientists have believed in let us go back in time some hundreds of years.

In 1486 a book was published. It was written in Latin and the original title was *Malleus Maleficarum*; the popular title was *Hexenhamer, The Witches' Hammer*, and the majority of the learned men, church dignitaries and judges of that day used this book as a guide. With the help of it tens of thousands of innocent women were tortured in the most atrocious manner and burnt at the stake, purportedly for being witches. Let me quote just one example of the sort of confession the torturers of the Inquisition obtained from these terribly abused women, with the help of that infamous book, confessions that were then used as evidence for their conviction by the judges of those days. It was stated that some witches were able to steal male organs from living men and to keep them alive in birds' nests in the woods by feeding them with worms.

One may laugh at these absurd beliefs, but some of the ideas

2

The body

and coincidences

propounded by our top scientists today are at least as preposterous. I will come back to that later in this book.

Seeing how wise our bodies are, it is not to be wondered at that the secret realm of coincidences can be observed in close connection with that very mysterious and wonderful instrument we inhabit all our lives and which is not something separate from us but an expression of ourselves.

My consulting room is situated on the east side of my house. When, during the winter, a strong, icy-cold wind blows from the east the water-pipe of my wash stand tends to freeze and in the 44 years we have lived in our house, I have not found another solution to this irritating problem other than waiting for the thaw to set in.

In the winter of 1980 it happened once again and I had to wash my hands, every time I had examined a patient, over on the west side of the house. I longed for the explosion with which the tap used to announce its start. On 24 February 1980 a mother came to me with her 6-year-old boy and asked me if I could help him. The problem was that he wet his bed every night. His bladder had not submitted to any night-training up till then and there were inundations of his bed at least once a night.

The words had hardly left her mouth when, behind me, there occurred the familiar explosion of the tap and then the water which I had not seen for two weeks began to spout with a vengeance.

Just as I have never been able to control that dratted tap, I was not able to cure the boy and just as I had to wait for the thaw, the mother had to wait for a couple of years before the boy spontaneously conquered his bedwetting.

There is something that every physician witnesses with a certain regularity and I presume that it also happens in other professions. The Germans call it "Duplizität der Fälle", the "doubling of cases", and the fact that it has a special name shows that this is a general phenomenon. Here is an example.

On 5 November 1996 I saw a woman in my office. I had treated her for a trigeminal neuralgia, which is a very painful inflammation of a nerve in the face. I asked her how she was and she answered, "Well, doctor, the pain has gone and I am very happy about that, but there is still a certain stiffness in my left cheek. It's kind of numb." I seldom see trigeminal neuralgia and have perhaps only treated 5 cases in 44 years, so I was rather relieved by this result.

The very next patient was a woman who had undergone an

operation for a brain tumour and come to me for complementary cancer treatment. I asked her how she was and she said, "Generally speaking, I am all right, doctor, but I have that stiff, numb feeling in my right cheek which is still a nuisance." She is the only woman I ever saw with that particular complaint after an operation.

So these two cases, happening one after the other, exhibiting the same sort of complaint, caused by different illnesses, and moreover a complaint of extreme rareness in my practice, are a beautiful demonstration of the "Duplizität". It belongs of course to the realm of coincidences, even if we have given a special name to it.

This story of the two women with the stiff, numb cheeks happened during a month when I was especially on the look-out for coincidences, as our Dutch-Flemish medical group had decided to assemble them in the period between two sessions and report on them at our next meeting. Such an agreement is practically an invitation for the phenomenon to explode. This was indeed what happened. While I usually note 2 to 3 cases a year, this time I noticed the phenomenon on 31 October, 2, 5, 6, 15, 16, 19, 20, 21 and 30 November, and 2 cases in December, making a total of 12. On 2 November a coincidence hit me really hard. I had been cutting wood for the fireplace and when I brought a basketful of it into the garage, I hit my head against a concrete beam, which is a bit low for my 6 feet 7 inches.

On that self-same day I was in my study and something fell on the floor. I bent to retrieve it, righted myself and hit my head very hard on exactly the same spot against a bookshelf that has been there for the last 25 years and never given me any trouble before. Perhaps the phenomenon wanted to point out to me that familiarity should never breed contempt.

Here is quite a different example relating to physical matters. Two years ago I saw for the first time a boy of nearly four, suffering from acute lymphatic leukaemia. He had received chemotherapy and corticosteroids and his white blood cell count was down. I questioned the parents about him and how they were coping with their child's severe illness. Because of the extremely dangerous nature of this illness I also asked them if they had any religion. To my surprise those two very Dutch-looking people with common Dutch names were devout Buddhists.

I looked at the little boy, sitting there stock-still on his mother's lap, staring at me with his almond-shaped eyes. The corticosteroids had given his face a full-moon shape. His fat little hands lay on his swollen little tummy. And suddenly it struck me that I was looking at a perfect little image of Buddha. There was no mistaking that fact. At least a year later, when I knew the parents better, I mentioned my first impression and they nodded in agreement.

"You are not the first one to say so," was their answer.

I was surprised how wise the little boy was and even more so when, as I heard, he talked quite openly about his possible death. He died in 1997, six years old.

AS CHANCE WOULD HAVE IT Sometimes one can wait for coincidences to happen.

I have a friend, a medical doctor, who always helps me in my practice on Wednesdays, doing the several tests we have reserved for that day of the week.

On a certain Wednesday he asked me at 9.45 a.m., "What exactly is meant by a calcarea carbonica child? I read the phrase somewhere and I do not understand it."

The expression comes from homoeopathy. Certain homoeopathic remedies are connected with certain physical distinguishing marks.

The pulsatilla child is described as fair-haired, plump, rosy-cheeked and prone to wilt in the first spell of hot weather.

The sulphur-type is described as lean, lank, hungry, and stoop-shouldered with an unwashed look.

The calcarea carbonica child is fat, fair, flabby, and pale. It is dumped in a chair and sits there, smiling around, sweating profusely in a cold room.

When you observe these characteristics, the related homoeopathic remedy is often indicated as the remedy of first choice.

I explained these types to my friend and said, "Wait, and one of these days I hope to show you a calcarea carbonica type of child."

We did not have to wait for long. A quarter-of-an-hour later a mother with a little girl arrived in my office. The girl was fat, pallid, and slightly sweating. She sat quietly on her mother's lap, looking around with a slow, friendly smile. That day was the first time I had seen her.

I called my friend who was busy with the tests and showed him the little girl.

"That is what I meant," I said.

Someone might ask, "How many calcarea carbonica children do you see a day? Three? Five?" As a matter of fact I am not a homoeopathic doctor and moreover most of the children I treat suffer from allergies. This means that they are usually very lively, even hyperactive, and often restless, so long as they have not been properly treated. The calcarea carbonica type is rare in my practice. Perhaps I see one every two months.

In the summer of 1995 something went wrong deep in my left under-jaw. There was an intermittent nasty pain, which kept me awake at night. The dentist could not find the cause at first but after some time, he discovered that, embedded deep in the jawbone, lay a wisdom tooth which was leaking and slowly decomposing. This meant the dental surgeon.

To appreciate the coincidence I am going to describe, a short explanation of the next part is necessary.

Man lives in symbols, he thinks in symbols and talks in symbols. When someone says: "That man is a swine", he of course does not mean it literally. The other person so indicated is not hobbling along on trotters and grunting, but behaves in a manner we humans think pigs would behave, if they were human.

A common symbol for the Russian State is the bear and for the USA a rather haggard-looking man, his hat adorned with the stars and stripes, called Uncle Sam.

Winston Churchill, the great leader in the Second World War, who represented all that was best in the UK (at least for us in the occupied countries, who saw in him the symbol of the coming liberation) looked uncommonly like the symbol of the British nation, John Bull.

One of the symbols for the human body is a house. Even people who are not aware of this fact can dream about a house and when you analyse the dream, it becomes clear that they are telling you something about their body. Jesus Christ also used a symbol for the human body like that, when he said: "Destroy this temple and in three days I will raise it up", meaning His body (John 2:19, 21). Paul also reminds us of the fact that our body is a temple (1 Cor. 6:19).

I have the impression that the more lofty symbol of the temple is used in the New Testament instead of a house, as the emphasis there lies on the Holy Spirit dwelling in the body, but for everyday psychology a house will do.

These symbols are not only active in our dreams and expressions but also around us, in daily life.

For some time during the summer of 1995 we had been having trouble in our hall. The ceiling light, a glass globe, slowly filled with water from time to time. As we had rather a lot of rain that summer, we first thought that one of the tiles on the roof had come loose, but when the water kept coming during a dry period, we asked the plumber to take a look.

So he broke up the floor on the first storey and found a needle-thin jet of water squirting from one of the pipes. Apparently, the condition had existed for a considerable time, as mushrooms were growing around it. So on that 13 September 1995 the plumber corrected the fault.

Please consider the situation: a plumber tearing up the floor with a lot of noise and finding a long-standing leak which was then repaired.

On 14 September 1995, a day later, I went to the Academic Hospital in Leyden and Professor Lekkas, an extremely capable and also amiable Greek gentleman, took one look at the x-rays my dentist had taken, shook his head, mumbling, "That's a nasty one", and, with the music of those encouraging words still in my ears, he laid me down in the dentist's chair we all know so well, gave me a local anaesthetic, took a sort of pneumatic drill and, with a horrible creaking noise, began to remove the offending leaking wisdom-tooth.

Look at the beautiful symmetry:

The whole summer, both my literal house and the house of my body suffered from a leak.

On 13 September, with much creaking, the floor was broken open in my literal house and the offending leak removed.

On 14 September the floor in my under-jaw was creakingly broken open and the leaking tooth was removed. An operation at my psychological house. Neither is this all.

The name of the surgeon who helped me so well was Professor Lekkas, a Greek name, but when you think of it as a Dutch name, it can be translated as follows:

Lek . . . a leak
Kas . . . a socket.

Here we hit upon another aspect of the strange phenomenon we are examining: it is fond of little jokes, puns and juggling with numbers. I will return to that subject later on.

On 5 January 1983 I was struck down with the nasty A 'flu, which hits you like a sledge-hammer. For a couple of days I was down and out but on the 9th I tottered down to the sitting-room.

"Look what I've found," my wife said with that bright healthy voice so rasping on the nerves of a convalescent 'flu patient. From an old, forgotten box some family films had emerged, one of them having been taken during our wedding in 1951.

We put on the film and there I was in my morning-coat and top hat, looking pale and haggard. Not the son-in-law I would have preferred. Why was I looking like that? Afraid of marriage? No, just before the wedding, I had been struck down by the Bornholm 'flu, an A virus of bad repute. My wedding feast had had to be postponed but on 9 July I had just recovered sufficiently to go through all the wedding ceremonies.

Look again at the symmetry:

3–8 July 1951   A 'flu
9 July 1951   Wedding
5–8 January 1983   A 'flu
9 January 1983   Film of wedding.

I had never seen that film before, by the way.

This structure is called alternation. In the 19th century one of the greatest biblical scholars of all Christian history, the Reverend E. W. Bullinger, discovered that the whole Bible was written according to this structure in combination with another one he called introversion.

Sometimes we can come across this beautiful structure in life.

On 18 September 1980 I awoke from a long and complicated dream. Only the last part lingered clearly in my mind and I wrote it down in my dream book. This was the dream:

I had a nasty pain in my throat and looked in the glass. My teeth were loose and I spat out some pieces of tooth, a stream of blood and finally a sharp piece of green glass, roughly in the shape of a triangle. I could feel the three places back in my throat, where the three points had been lodged.

I jumped out of my bed and looked in the mirror and to my intense relief I found everything all right, but still that morning the dream kept coming back to me, troubling my mind.

It was a Thursday and on that day I always take an hour's walk in the sand dunes nearby, directly after finishing my first consulting hour. It is a beautiful piece of wild nature, with many sorts of birds, two sorts of deer, foxes and many different plants. While I walked there that morning I was still pondering my dream. Whatever did it mean? The blood from my mouth, the triangular piece of green glass. . . . Was it a warning of an impending disease? Suddenly it struck me that the nose tonsil and the two throat tonsils lay in a triangle and at once I was transported back in time. I was six years old and being taken to a hospital in Haarlem. There I was put in the lap of a huge male nurse with a rubber apron, who took me in a iron grip.

Around the corner came Dr E in a white coat and he carried in his right hand what looked like pruning shears. I had to open my mouth wide and then I felt a pain more horrible than anything I had ever experienced. In a stream of blood I spat out two red, round balls. In 1931 anaesthetic for such a minor operation was not thought necessary.

I now understand why that dream had troubled me at this particular moment. The previous evening my wife had asked me, "Please drive over to your mother, dear, and fetch the pruning shears, I need to do something about the hedge tomorrow morning."

Pleased with myself at having found that chain of associations – Pruning shears . . . dream . . . Dr E . . . tonsil operation with sort of pruning shears – I hit something with my next step which tinkled slightly. I bent down to see what it was and there, just in front of my right foot, in the sand on top of the dune where I was walking, lay a triangular piece of green glass, exactly like the one I had spat out that morning in my dream. Hamlet certainly would have said something deep about it to Horatio. I was about 50 when Dr E (by the way, a very sweet man when you knew him better) died in my arms vomiting blood from a burst artery in his oesophagus. I was his physician for many years and I had grown quite fond of this good-natured and unassuming old specialist.

It is strange how I spat blood during our first encounter and he vomited blood during our last one.

The piece of green triangular glass is still in my possession. I took it home with me and it occupies pride of place between my crystals and shells.

AFTER HAVING GIVEN the reader 12 stories to illustrate what I mean by coincidence, let us sit back and think for a moment.

Most people will be able to supplement these histories with their own experiences. Coincidences are common phenomena in the human race and they must have been observed ever since man first walked the earth. Early in history, humanity must have realised that there lay a tremendous potential in the phenomenon and will have wondered if it were possible to harness it in order to serve human purposes.

In this chapter I will give an example of how humanity strove to accomplish this aim. This chapter must be considered as an intermezzo between stories. More of these intermezzos are to follow and each time I will give an example of the harnessing of coincidence. Here I will talk about astrology.

Not, however, the astrology you read in the papers, promising you a romantic interlude on Wednesday and some financial windfall on Friday. Let us keep it serious.

When a person is born, astrologers make use of the principle of coincidence. Here, on the one hand, is the new-born baby, there, on the other hand, is the great clock of heaven. Astrology says that there exists a meaningful relationship between the two. The astrologers say that they are able to read the great clock of the stars and in so doing are enabled to read the character and much of the future of a person. They also say that by being able to read those things they can help a person along his sometimes wearisome path.

Why is this making use of the phenomenon of coincidence?

Because two seemingly unrelated sequences "fall together", to wit, the tracks of the stars and the path of life of an individual. However these two sequences of events (stars above and life-events below) are brought together in a meaningful relationship.

The great difference from spontaneous coincidence is that, in the case of astrology, the astrologer more or less forces the meaningful relationship to be there. It all depends on the interpreter, and between one astrologer and another one the differences in interpretation are great.

Now, happily, every person is a mystery and the heavenly clock is as silent as the grave about a person's essence. Only the good Lord knows who we really are, astrology never.

One could call this a maxim: astrology can never tell who a person is. On the other hand it can tell you a lot about what a person *has*, his abilities and capacities. Here the phenomenon of coincidence appears to have a direct practical application.

3

1st Intermezzo
Astrology

Now I will not talk about astrology in its usual sense as it is practised by professional astrologers. I shall only comment on a certain rather specialised part of it, a part moreover less known to the general public.

As everyone knows, the earth revolves around the sun, describing a full circle in a year, and this movement is responsible for the sun seemingly having a different starry background every month. On 21 March the sun will be in that part of the starry heavens called Ram, and then month by month move through Taurus, Gemini and the rest of the signs of the zodiac until it reaches the final sign of the Fishes.

Every sign has thirty degrees of the zodiacal circle. Although the 12 signs are known to nearly everyone, it is less widely known that every degree is connected as well with a picture or, rather, two pictures. The first series was assembled by a French "Professor of Astrology" in Paris (whatever that title may be worth) called J. Duzéa, who writes under the name of Janduz.

Every single one of those pictures is of a certain problem to be solved in life. We do not know for certain where these pictures come from. They may be very old or not so very old. In any case they are beautifully drawn in Janduz's book, set in the 18th century. As there are no steam engines in it, but there are sorting-rifles, I place them in the middle of the 18th century. It is possible that the original pictures are far older and that they have been modernised, just as Shakespeare is sometimes played in a modern setting with jazz music and 20th-century costume (always give me the genuine presentation, as in the splendid BBC renderings).

The second series has been published in the USA as far as I know and has been "seen" by a clairvoyant sitting evening after evening in one of New York's parks, if I am rightly informed.

These pictures in the second series are less down to earth and are said to give solutions to the first series, picture by picture. They have been published in a book by a French astrologer called Dane Rudhyar.

All this information I received from a rather famous Dutch astrologer, who at the end of his life lived in Glastonbury, England, by the name of Wim Koppejan. His life's work was immense research into these 720 pictures and an attempt to demonstrate from the lives of well-known people how they worked. It was he who said that the second series was the solution to the first one. The whole picture gallery was published in 1990 with Koppejan's commentaries, by his wife, Helene von Woelderen. I have the Dutch edition but I do not know if there is an English one too.

Let me now give you some examples of how this picture gallery can be used.

I had a young woman in my practice, aged 18, who was rather in revolt against the fate that had turned her life sour.

Her younger brother had been an invalid from an early age. His illness was called muscular dystrophy and he was in a wheelchair, unable to walk and barely able to lift his arms. He had to be helped all the time and this young woman wanted to go out and have fun just like her friends, when, in fact, much of her spare time was taken up with helping her brother.

"Why me?" she asked me.

I looked in the ephemeris of the planets' places for her day of birth and found that her sun, the most important heavenly body in the chart, stood in the 17th degree of Gemini.

This degree is depicted as a man sitting in a chair, wearing a dressing-gown, stretching out both his arms towards a table laden with nice books, pencils, all sorts of fruit and other desirable things, unable to reach them as he has no hands. The word going with this degree is "impotence".

When I showed her this picture, she received a shock, because she recognised the situation confronting her all day long, but that was not the main reason for the shock. She realised that it was not a degree in her brother's chart she was looking at, but one in her own. She suddenly saw that, apparently, the situation belonged to her and that she would never escape it by rebelling against it. You might as well try and rebel against your own legs. One way or another she had to transform the situation instead of trying to escape from it.

Of course this didn't make the situation easier, but the new insight helped her to change her negative attitude to a more positive one.

The second, "higher" picture, the one that is meant to solve the problem posed by the first one, demonstrated the necessity of a ripening process to perfection. It said: "Head of a youth changes into that of a mature thinker."

A second example of what can be done with the pictures is this. First, a "situation sketch".

During our clinical training we medical students had to stay for one month in a big house in Leyden during the last stages of our studies. We were on call there for the deliveries of babies, first in hospital and afterwards in town.

Two of my friends there were Corrie and Tom, recently married.

One evening when we were waiting for the things or, rather babies, to come, calling us out on duty, Tom asked me, "Is your wife pregnant already?"

In those times, long past, you married and had children.

"No," I said, "not yet."

"Neither is Corrie," he said. "What about making a bet and seeing whose wife gets pregnant first or, rather whose child will be born first?"

"Tom, stop it!" his wife exclaimed, highly scandalised. We were the last generation educated by Victorian parents.

One of the other students present at this conversation, a certain Herman, looked at this bet from a practical viewpoint.

"You'd first have to attune their cycles," he remarked drily.

Within a month both wives were pregnant. Corrie was so convinced that Tom's crazy proposition had given her a shock, that she initially thought it was a false pregnancy, but both the children were for real and my wife and Corrie both produced beautiful boys, ours winning the race by three days.

Both boys became medical doctors. It would have been strange if it had turned out otherwise.

Tom became a general practitioner in a friendly village on a river in the eastern part of our country and I settled as a GP in Haarlem, near the west coast.

Some years later my wife and I decided to pay a visit to our old friends from our days in Leyden, so we drove to the east.

We arrived at the river and a little ferry-boat brought us in our car to the other side.

The car climbed the road leading up the embankment and we looked down at the village with its church and its red roofs and the orchards around it.

"I wonder where they live," my wife said.

I had halted the car and pointed down at a beautiful white house.

"Over there," I said.

"However do you know?" she exclaimed. "You've never been here before, have you?"

"That house is exactly the picture of the 18th degree of Libra, and it is the principal one in the Chart of Little Hugo," I said.

We drove down the village street, turned a corner and there was the house in front of us and there were our friends expecting us.

The word belonging to the picture was "hospitality".

In the years to come our family was to learn how true this was.

A third example happened when I had just graduated from university. I had a couple of months left before I had to do my national service, which was still compulsory. Every dictator leaves something bad behind him and in Napoleon's case it was compulsory national service in our country. It ceased in 1996. During those months left to me, I worked in a psychiatric hospital under a doctor whose name was Nic.

I was assigned to the female ward. There was one patient who could only be kept in an isolation cell. This was in 1952, before strong tranquillizers changed the whole psychiatric scene.

When you looked through the bars into her padded cell, you could see this woman, Mrs L, striding up and down like a caged tiger, lashing out at the bars from time to time and growling.

When she had to be washed, at least four nurses rushed into her cell and grabbed part of the patient, an arm or a leg, holding on to it for dear life, because she was extremely violent.

For new, young assistants the staff had a sort of initiation rite. My turn came when one afternoon I was told, "Tomorrow morning you go to Mrs L and have a little talk with her."

I did not sleep well that night and with a hollow feeling in the pit of my stomach I went to the hospital. I was so confused (or my subconscious was so wise) that I went and interviewed another patient, an elderly and totally submissive frail little woman.

The head nurse soon found the truant and with a sweet voice in which the smirk was clearly audible she said, "That is not Mrs L, Doctor."

She and Dr Nic led me full of expectation to Mrs L's cell and watched me with knowing smiles as I walked into Mrs L's lair.

There was one thing, however, they did not realise. I had a trump card up my sleeve. That morning I had looked up the degree where the sun of Mrs L stood, as I knew her birthday from her file.

I had discovered that this was the 13th degree of Aquarius.

The picture was that of a very angry lion, lashing out against the bars of its iron cage. "Anarchist" was the word belonging to the picture. I was astonished at the way the 13th degree of Aquarius depicted Mrs L in her isolation cell.

I had also looked up the higher degree and read: "A barometer hangs under the porch of a quiet rural inn."

When I entered the cell the only thing I could contrive to do was to concentrate on the serene picture of the rural inn. There I stood before the dreaded patient. She was a regal person, well built, about forty, with a handsome face, big searching eyes and black hair. When she saw me, she took a step backwards and stood absolutely still, her head a little bit tilted back, and scrutinized me intensely. Suddenly she drew a ring from her finger, made a courteous bow and offered it to me.

"Take it," I heard Nic hissing beyond the half-open door.

I took the ring and I believe I spoke some soothing words to the patient before leaving the padded cell. I felt light-headed and extremely relieved.

In the corridor my superior greeted me with the words, "Blast it, how did you manage that?"

I kept silent but later on, when the head nurse had gone and we were in his room, I told him about it. From that moment on we became friends and a friendship began that has lasted until today and hopefully will remain intact for the rest of our lives.

I could give many more examples of the way these pictures are interwoven with the web of human lives, but it is not necessary.

From my experiences with them, I slowly began to understand that it is not only the body of a person that appears when he or she is born. The circumstances are born with the person, they are part of the personality, and when someone grows up, the circumstances unfold slowly, one after the other.

Often one hears people complaining, "If only the circumstances of my life had been better . . . "

Well, they are not because the borders of a personality do not stop at the skin. The circumstances belong to the totality of the individual and trying to change them from the outside often only changes them for the worse.

How many times does one not see someone changing a partner, only to find himself or herself with a partner possessing exactly the same or at least similar traits as the former one!

A real change of circumstances can only be achieved from within. A change in attitude literally performs miracles.

Let me give an example to illustrate this point.

One day my wife wanted to see wild deer. They were at that time extremely rare in the dunes, so we went to a part of our country where they are still seen in abundance, called the "Hoge Veluwe".

We asked the gamekeeper where deer could be found and he recommended us three places. We visited them all but found no trace of deer.

"We are going about this in the wrong way," I said to my wife.

"Now let us just take a walk. We are going to forget the right places and stroll over this wide open field of heather and think deer, talk deer, in short, the whole deer and nothing but the deer. By the way, what do you know about deer?"

We engaged in conversation about these beautiful and gracious animals and kept at it for about ten minutes. Then I said, "Now look right in front of you."

There, about 50 yards away from us stood a deer, suckling two young. We stood looking at the lovely sight for quite some time and then, just behind these animals, along came at least 50 deer, bounding along at a great rate. They jumped and ran, jumped again, with long, almost floating, movements. They came from the right and went to the left. Never before nor ever after have I seen so many deer at the same time in my life.

A change in our attitude had given us the sight we had longed for.

When one knows the pictures in one's own gallery it is a strange feeling to witness them being acted out in the exterior world, as happens from time to time. You are suddenly inside your own picture and it is a humbling experience because then you become aware of being part of an unfathomable whole, far bigger than you can understand.

In my view, though, there is a definite danger in astrology. I have a feeling that the extremely mobile world of coincidences does not like to be harnessed. It likes to be free, bubbling, and sparkling, like a waterfall or an ever-changing cloud, never the same from one moment to the next. Pinning this world down can lead to arrogance and price. Apart from the incident with Mrs L, I never again used a magical gimmick like that. It just did not feel right. It does not become man to play God.

Is it right to relate the phenomenon of coincidences to astrology?

To a normal scientific mind, relating stars in the heavens to men on earth is just playing with coincidental places of the stars and haphazardly binding them to men's lives. In the case of the pictures the whole business is even more complicated. Someone (who?) started the idea that certain pictures of unknown origin belonged to the 360 degrees of the zodiac and when this was established, a completely coincidental game one could say, these pictures were related to people's birthdays on our planet earth, thus creating a series of coincidences within another series of coincidences. The maddening thing is that, for some reason or other, the results are not total rubbish, but meaningful events. If this is not a good example of the mystery of coincidence, I wonder what is.

As concerns astrology in my own life, I regularly made astrological charts of my patients when I was still a young GP. In the long run, however, I noticed that the horoscope inserted itself between myself and my patient. I saw them "through" their horoscopes, instead of directly. They became a type instead of a human being.

I have seen how this attitude can lead the astrologist to a severe form of pride, a sort of God Almighty complex. I discarded astrology because I discovered that I had to experience my patients in a direct way. Some simple questions and an attitude of empathy give you more insight, and work more quickly and certainly, than complicated astrological calculations.

The astrological phase in my life was interesting as long as it lasted, but there are far better ways of approaching your fellow human beings. No one *is* a lion or a scorpion. They are only part of your inner zoo of which you are the director.

The animals living there can be tamed and are then very helpful. Let me give you the tale of an adventure with some inner animals.

What I am going to relate here has nothing to do with astrology.

I always admire strong silent men. When they suffer, they suffer alone and show a brave front to the world. I've hardly ever met one outside Hollywood films, by the way. Strong silent sufferers are usually women. Men bawl their heads off when something goes wrong. I belong in that category.

In April 1986 a nasty insidious pain began to nag me day and night. As it was situated in my cheek, I went to the dentist who meant to encourage me with the uplifting message that my teeth were not the culprits. Immediately, two internal demons began to rear their ugly heads. One whispered with an unholy smile that it was a particularly unpleasant form of arthritis in the mandibular joint, while the other with an evil leer whispered that a tumour was growing at a fast rate. As these two laid on an alternating 24-hour service, I got pretty fed up.

As normal procedures did not turn up the reason for the pain, I decided upon an experiment. I chose three animals from my inner zoo and set them in front of me. To the elephant I said, "You are a sick tooth." He nodded. To the hedgehog I said, "You are a rheumatic joint." He turned up his nose. To the crocodile, "You are a tumour." He wagged his tail.

I added a knitting needle for trigeminal neuralgia and after this guaranteed unscientific procedure I waited. This happened on the morning of 30 April 1986.

At 6 o'clock that afternoon I was waiting for the television news, when an advertisement flashed up on the screen. As with most advertisements, I no longer know which product was being recommended, but what I saw was first a very small fake crocodile and then the silhouette of a very real elephant.

Interpreting the answer of my brave animals, I decided that the tumour scare was false but that some tooth was the culprit.

Later that evening I read a book called *If This be Magic* by Guy Lion Playfair and there was a story about a lantern-fly pretending to be a crocodile to scare the creatures around him.

This clinched the matter and I went back to the dentist who took an x-ray and found an inflammation at the root of a tooth.

The tumour idea had just been a scare, no more, but the elephant could be found as a silhouette in the x-ray.

Do not ask me how these things work. Coincidences are playful. Invite them in and they begin to frolic around you.

Astrology can be fun but, for heaven's sake, do not take it seriously. Human beings are never ruled by the stars unless they let them.

IN THIS SMALL chapter I will give some examples of coincidences being tied up with animals. The last chapter about the zodiac and deer and elephants was a preamble to this one.

The phenomenon we are studying, which we call for lack of a better word "coincidence", loves animals. It is sad that they can not appreciate the way in which they play a role in chance happenings. Most higher animals love a certain amount of fun and would love to share the joke.

On 30 March 1985 I happened upon an illustrated magazine and there I found absolutely gorgeous fake pictures of unicorns. A majestic white unicorn galloping along, two unicorns in a flowery meadow, a unicorn swimming. I instantly fell in love with them, cut them out and glued them in my diary.

In all my (nearly) 60 years I had never had anything to do with unicorns. I had not come across them or collected them, or read about them. I only knew what the name meant and that there was a mill of that name in Haarlem, next to the old (and now canalised) river. I also knew a fellow GP in Bloemendaal called Eenhoorn, the Dutch for unicorn.

The year went on and I forgot about the unicorns again.

That year in November my youngest son brought home a beautiful girl, whom I loved at first sight and who later became a dear daughter-in-law.

When at the end of that year – as I always do – I went slowly through my diary to mark the main events, I first hit upon the unicorns and again admired the fairy tale-like quality of the pictures before coming to the November meeting with Pauline whose maiden name was, as you will by now have gathered, Eenhoorn, "Unicorn", a niece of my colleague from many years ago. Her arrival had cast a long shadow in advance, or should I say that the law of coincidence had provided a signature tune to announce her arrival in our family?

Let me move on to another example.

There exists a hidden illness that is often not recognised. It is a very slight but very real hypofunction of the thyroid. Women especially tend to be victims. Sometimes the laboratory tests do not show any aberration but Barnes, in his book, *Hypothyroidism, the Unexpected Illness*, has taught me that all the same the illness may be there. The way to determine this is by taking your morning temperature for a week just before rising in the morning (thermometer under armpit).

A mean basal temperature below 36.6°C (= 98°F) is suspect.

The complaints can be various, but often the patients tell you that they cannot get warm.

In 1991 I advised one of my patients to take her basal temperature for a week.

On 12 May she had her next appointment. As the previous patient had taken less time than expected, I had to wait five minutes. At that time I was reading a book written by Maartje van Tijn, a Jewish woman, about the Exodus. I opened this book and read about the great plague of frogs in Egypt, one of the ten plagues that brought Egypt to its knees. *Midraggim II* the book was called and for a short time I was absorbed in frogs. I recalled how, during a summer vacation on Terschelling, we had played the Exodus, with our family and how, on the "frog day" the children had cut frogs from green paper and hidden them everywhere in the house.

Then time was up and I opened the file of the next patient, the one who had been taking her basal temperature. I saw that my assistant had attached a card to the file. It was something my patient had written to me. She had drawn a large green frog and written, "This is the temperature chart of T, the cold frog. And this when I do not feel anything for frogs. Kind Regards." The chart indeed revealed an under-active thyroid.

I do not know if the next small story, more an observation really, belongs to the realm of coincidences. You judge for yourself.

In my neighbourhood there lived an old and slightly decrepit woman. She had difficulty with walking and when she slowly moved along the square, which she did every day, she put one leg in front of her and then drew the other leg level with the first one. She was a plump, pale woman.

She was always accompanied by a small, plump, white dog of uncertain breed, who walked very close to her. A remarkable thing about that dog was that it walked on three legs and hardly used one of its hind legs, which made rather vague movements just above street level. There they stumbled along, two of a kind.

Is this coincidence? I wonder. Jo Spier, one of our gifted illustrators before the war, once drew a series of pictures of dogs with the masters in the Saturday paper and wrote under them only: "Have you noticed this too?"

All these dogs looked like their masters, or the masters like their dogs. Didn't Churchill have a bulldog?

We are gods to animals. Perhaps they model themselves after our image when they know us long enough.

One day a woman living in Amsterdam came to my office. I had known her for a long time, as she had been a girl in my practice in Haarlem many years ago. She was now in her thirties and she wanted some advice about getting her body into the best possible condition. This was because, up until then, she had not been able to become pregnant.

Her gynaecologist had advised her to try in vitro fertilisation, what we call test-tube babies. The waitinglist in Amsterdam for this technique, however, was one year and she did not want to wait that long, so she found a place in Belgium at the Academic Hospital in Leuven. There she could be helped after only three weeks. First came the usual preparation with injections, and then she went to Leuven for the implantation of an egg, fertilised with the sperm of her husband.

When everything had been done the doctor said to her, "I advise you to stay in a hotel in Leuven tonight. Do not go back to Amsterdam till tomorrow."

Like a notice on a bottle: "Don't shake".

My patient, however, absolutely refused to do this.

"We have a comfortable car and we will drive slowly back to Amsterdam," she said.

So off they went, through Belgium and the south of the Netherlands. Nearing the great bridge called the Moerdijk, she suddenly cried out, "Look at that!"

There, straight at their car, flew a magnificent stork, nearly diving onto their roof and then floating away again.

"It has succeeded!" she said with great certainty to her husband.

Nowadays, children are confronted at a very tender age with the facts of life through our candid TV programmes, but still in the subconscious of humanity lives on that old tale our grandmothers told their children, that babies were brought by the stork.

Indeed, 9 months later, a beautiful girl was born, now growing up into a very determined young lady, who rules her family with a gentle but decisive hand.

Apparently there is more to the story of the stork than meets the eye.

IN THE PART about astrology I showed how certain images, call them archetypes if you like, a term coined by Jung, are connected with the 360 degrees of the zodiac, and how these images seem to belong to a person from birth, according to the places of the heavenly bodies in the degrees at the exact time of birth.

In every life at least 12 images, connected with the sun, moon, 9 planets, rising sign and "commission in life", are co-incidental with the moment of birth and, according to those who have studied the subject "colour" the entire life of a person. Is this coincidence?

This is a difficult question. Some would say that it is indeed pure coincidence to be born on a certain date and at a certain hour and so these images that colour life are no more than auto-suggestion, self-fulfilling prophecies.

Others, who believe in the unity of all that exists, will say that when a new personality appears on earth, it is not a haphazard occurrence, but connected with that particular "seed moment" and part of the specific conditions of heaven and earth at the time.

I am aware of the fact that I slightly repeat myself, but this is on purpose. We are analysing coincidences and the problem must be set out as clearly as possible. Is coincidence chance or might there be design in it? That is the question we have to solve in this book. And also: what exactly *is* coincidence?

"Primitive" peoples, for instance, have more feeling for the unity of this world than the "civilised" town-dweller of the 20th century. They will express this feeling by calling a new-born child "Flying Eagle" or "Stamping Bull", if these animals manifested themselves in that way at its time of birth. Later on they will notice the character of the child mirroring those names. Something of this feeling for meaningful connections even lingers on in many of us. I remember back in the thirties the great Melbourne race, the first famous race for airplanes. There were two categories: those who raced to Melbourne hell for leather (won, if my memory serves me right, by a British team) and the handicap race, in which certain stops were obligatory, for passenger planes, won by a KLM plane, Uiver (an old-fashioned word for stork). I do not remember where the race started, London or Amsterdam, but I do remember the whole of our country being glued to the radio and, when the Uiver won, how a couple with a new-born baby called their child "Uivertje" (little Uiver). I have often wondered what became of her. A stewardess perhaps?

Once more returning to astrology: as the images belonging to a person can be calculated with the help of a good ephemeris, one

5

2nd Intermezzo
The
I Ching

could say that this is "calculated coincidence", which of course is a contradiction in terms, a paradox even. It must be clear that we are not talking about a direct cause-and-effect law, and yet we seem to discern a definite connection. It is all very mysterious.

The difficulty is that the 19th-century science, which still dominates our thinking, puts great emphasis on physical scientific laws, those connected with repeatable experiments, statistics, exact measurements, double-blind tests and so on. While this is all right in itself, it excludes all other phenomena and this is tunnel vision, because natural laws are only part of the picture.

There are at least three different sorts of laws, and probably a lot more categories, but let us restrict ourselves to those three:

I. The physical laws studied by modern scientists, which we can discover by careful observation and indeed often discover in a painful way as children, such as the law of gravity. I fall from a ladder and break a leg. We know that law from direct experience; it is Newton who gave the law its scientific formulation.

And there is the law of preservation of energy. The total amount of energy in a closed system stays the same. Though this law has been formulated in a scientific way only in this scientific age, we all know it very well from experience: when I drink my coffee too hot, I burn my mouth.

All physical laws are explained nowadays in scientific terms.

II. The spiritual laws, indirectly experienced, pertaining to the soul. People cannot discover them through careful observation. They are moral laws and must be revealed. The Ten Commandments are a good example.

Transgression of these laws damages the eternal soul but more often than not, nothing of this hurt can be observed with the senses. Even Job in one of the oldest books of the Old Testament complained:

> "The tents of robbers prosper,
> and they that provoke God are secure." (Job 12:6)

And also

> "Wherefore do the wicked live,
> become old, yea wax mighty in power?
> Their seed is established in their sight with them
> and their offspring before their eyes,
> their houses are safe without fear,
> neither is the rod of God upon them." (Job 21:7–9)

An important part of Job is preoccupied with this enigma: good men encounter evil, bad men fare well.

In our time Harold S. Kushner has written the book *When Bad Things Happen to Good People*.

In other words: laws like the Ten Commandments must be believed and bring their own recompense with them, but hidden in the soul, where no one can see them. They are not laws in the physical sense. They are not "scientific" according to our way of thinking and that is why many people, especially those who believe in "historic materialism", think that these laws can be discarded and that the aim always justifies the means.

III. Recently, a third set of laws has been formulated, the so-called "non-linear" ones. They can be found, if one looks for them, but they do not seem to follow the logical and orderly sequence of category I, nor to have the invisible effects of category II.

For example, Colborn, Dumanoski and Myers, in their book *Our Stolen Future*, explain how an estrogen-like substance, a pollutant produced by the plastic industry, floating around in our environment, can play havoc with our health, giving rise to birth deformities, especially of the reproductive organs and, later in life, cause certain cancers.

But – and this is the new idea pointing towards another set of laws – these compounds are not always detrimental to human beings. They only do their dirty work during a certain short period of gestation. The writers talk about "a window in time".

Another example has recently been given by Professor Schatz, the discoverer of streptomycin.

He has stated that certain poisons *above* a certain concentration follow the linear scientific law of exposure, i.e. the more poison, the sicker the exposed person.

However, *below* that critical level, something unexpected happens. At some low concentrations the poison does not seem to have any effect, but then at even lower concentrations, it suddenly appears to be very dangerous indeed. Thus an undulating curve is found, with slowly decreasing concentrations which are sometimes neutral, sometimes dangerous.

Schatz takes as an example the toxicity of fluoride, a poison with about the strength of arsenic. Fluoride poisoning forms a linear poisoning curve above a certain concentration, but an undulating non-linear one below it. The 1 p.p.m. concentration used for the fluoridation of water supplies intended to reduce tooth decay is precisely such a dangerous concentration and explains the 10%

higher death rate from cancer in fluoridated cities, which is often not found in animal tests using higher concentrations.*

L. Kolisko in Germany has demonstrated these undulating curves with a great variety of metal salts, using ever higher dilutions to germinate gladiolus seeds in and then observing a rhythm in growing and flowering inhibitions and enhancements.

It could well be that the phenomenon we call coincidence is related to this third category of laws. Sometimes they suddenly occur, forming real clusters, when circumstances are favourable, and sometimes they do not show themselves at all.

There exists one people on our planet that has studied the law of coincidence – if I may be permitted to use this expression – to perfection: the Chinese.

Their *I Ching*, or *Book of Changes*, is a gold-mine for anyone who wants to know more about the mysterious world of coincidence, and has been a source of inspiration for more than 2000 years in China. Confucius, the great Chinese sage, studied this book intensively and at the end of his life regretted that he had not another 50 years left to study the *I Ching*.

Even more than astrology the *I Ching* seems to have mastered the art of letting coincidence speak for itself. For those who do not know anything about it, I will give a short explanation.

Imagine you are Chinese and you have a problem. You have a choice, for instance, between studying law or medicine.

You are a good Chinese and do not go to a psychological institute where they test you on your capabilities but to an expert on the *I Ching*. This man does not follow the Western pattern, doing all sorts of smart tests like Rorschach and what not, but he takes three coins, shakes them in his hand, throws them on the table and notes down what he sees.

This he repeats six times. For heads he notes the number 3, for tails the number 2. Now there are 4 possible outcomes for each throw:

Heads-heads-heads: $3 + 3 + 3 = 9$.
Heads-heads-tails: $3 + 3 + 2 = 8$.
Heads-tails-tails: $3 + 2 + 2 = 7$.
Tails-tails-tails: $2 + 2 + 2 = 6$.

An even number (6 and 8) is drawn as a broken line: - -.
An odd number (7 and 9) is drawn as a continuous line: —.

* *Fluoride, Journal of the International Society for Fluoride Research*, Volume 30, number 2, May 1997, pages 131–133.

Beginning at the lowest level, a symbol is built up of six broken or continuous lines, one above the other. So the lowest line is called the first line, the highest the sixth line.

It looks, for instance, like this one:

☷

The symbol is called a hexagram.

There are 64 possibilities.

Each of these 64 possibilities has a name, such as "Peace", "The Cooking Pot", "The Unfathomable".

These words are explained in what is called "The Judgement". For instance, in hexagram 48, "The Well", the judgement is" "One can relocate the town but not the well. It does not decrease, it does not increase. They come and go and draw from the well. When one has nearly reached the water but the rope is just not long enough, or when the pitcher breaks, it brings misfortune."

Apart from this judgement there is also an image. Not a drawn image, it is described in words. For The Well it is:

"Above the wood is the water, the image of the well. So the noble man encourages the people at work and admonishes them to help each other."

All very Chinese.

Not too difficult when one knows the 64 hexagrams, one could say, but wait.

Sixes and nines are called "moving" lines. They change into their opposite, thus giving rise to another hexagram. One can see in which direction a certain situation tends to move.

This of course increases the amount of possibilities enormously.

The lines with the number 6 or 9 are so important that they each have a special significance. For instance, staying with The Well:

"6 at the beginning = the mud of the well is not drunk. Animals don't come to an old well."

This again increases the amount of possibilities even more, which in the end leads to very individual readings.

One could be completely wrong to assume that the *I Ching* is just a way to foretell the future, like a gipsy gazing into a crystal ball at a fair.

The *I Ching* is one of the greatest books of wisdom in the world. Reading it, a Christian is reminded of the book of Proverbs in the Old Testament or the apocryphal Book of Wisdom.

The advice given in these two books is essentially the same as that in the *I Ching*, with one important difference.

43

First let us look at the similarities. "He that guardeth his mouth keepeth his life; but for him that openeth wide his lips there shall be ruin." (Prov. 13:3)

Compare this to hexagram 27, "Nutrition". "At the foot of the mountain there is thunder, the image of food. Thus the noble man guards his words and is modest in eating and drinking."

And later the text says: "The culture of silence sees to it that words coming out of the mouth don't exceed their measure and that food coming into the mouth does not exceed its measure. Thus character is formed."

Compare this with the New Testament: "If any man offend not in words, the same is a perfect man and is able to bridle the whole body.

3. Behold, we put bits in the horses mouths that they may obey us and we turn about their whole body.

4. Behold, also the ships, which though they be so great and are driven of fierce winds yet are they turned about with very small helm withersoever the governor listeth." (James 3:2)

One can easily see that the advice concerning speech is the same in Proverbs, the *I Ching* and James.

Now for the difference.

A person consulting Proverbs or James might think, "This does not apply to me" or "This looks a bit like my own situation at the moment."

A person consulting the *I Ching* gets the answer, "This, at this particular moment, is your position."

The *I Ching* shows us another dimension and, using the law of coincidence, advises the person seeking help what to do, or (this is very important in the *I Ching*) what to refrain from at this particular moment in life.

A Christian with a living faith does not need to use a technique like this. During his morning prayer he will hear, if necessary, the Holy Spirit telling him the Biblical text that can be directly applied to the situation, or be given another sort of indication as to what he should do.

The majority of people on this planet are not Christians, though, and the good Lord has not let them flounder without guidance. Every people on earth has received some form of revelation and the Chinese have been blessed by this book full of wisdom. It is also full of common sense, and it need not be used as a direct guide in trouble, but just for the strengthening of character.

As concerns common sense, look for instance at the commentary for the first line of the hexagram "Encounter". "A meagre swine also has its swine's nature."

Certain Christian circles tend to charge with heresy books like the *I Ching*, imagining them to have sprung directly from Satan.

Let them look at hexagram 59, "The solution". "The wind blows over the water, the image of the solution. So the old kings sacrificed to their Lord and built their temples."

This sounds like monotheism, and did not Jesus also talk about the wind blowing where it wills? (John 3: 8). He applied it to those being born from the Spirit.

It is not exactly the same but look at what the commentary also says in this part of the *I Ching*: "Egoism and greed isolate people. This is why a pious affection has to conquer their hearts. They have to be saved by a shudder of awe in the face of Eternity, that gives them as in a flash of lightning an intuitive comprehension of the Only Creator of all living creatures and unites them through the power of community feelings at the holy ceremony of worshipping God."

So the old Chinese made use of what Jung later called synchronicity, different and seemingly unrelated things happening at the same time, forming a new synthesis. It is not surprising that, when Richard Wilhelm for the first time translated the *I Ching* into a Western language, Professor C. G. Jung wrote the introduction.

A great many years ago one of my patients came to my office. She had always been a sturdy girl and never had anything more than a slight cold or 'flu. She was now 16 years old and she told me that suddenly she had developed a nameless fear. I asked her if something had happened recently which could have caused this complaint, but she answered that it had come out of the blue. I was very busy at that time, with many patients waiting, so I asked her to return some days later, when I would have time for her and we could have a long talk. In the meantime I told her to think back over the last months and try to remember if anything out of the ordinary had happened to her.

When she came back three days later, she had something interesting to report.

Six weeks ago there was a gap in her memory. She remembered going on her bicycle to her cello lesson and some hours later being at home and having a telephone conversation with a friend. In-between, nothing.

In itself it was interesting that she remembered such a gap. That meant that there was something under pressure in her soul.

We talked for a while but the black gap remained, so I could not come up with a better idea other than to put her under hypnosis. First

45

I ascertained the exact day and hour when the gap had occurred and then I put her into a state of deep relaxation.

I took her back to the moment she had left home and mounted her bicycle. This time the mist lifted and she described to me how she had arrived at the house of her cello teacher, called "Uncle John", as he was an old friend of the family.

He told her that he had just bought a new and beautiful cello, took her upstairs to show it to her and tried to rape her. She fought back with teeth and nails and escaped from the house, but the shock had completely blocked her memory. This is perhaps difficult to understand, but Uncle John was not just a cello teacher. She had grown up with him in the neighbourhood, a trusted and beloved person.

At this moment, I was confronted with a difficult decision: I could give her back her memory, but did not know what this new shock would do to her. Or I could cover up everything, leaving the memory simmering in the depths, until perhaps it emerged spontaneously. In the meantime I could give her some soothing counter-suggestions.

I decided to take the chance, though it was risky. Hypnosis is sometimes like an operation and should never be undertaken lightly. I told her that, when she woke up, she would remember everything. I brought her out of her hypnotic trance, she looked at me a bit groggily, and then suddenly I saw memory flooding her mind. She sat up with a jerk and exclaimed, "The scoundrel!"

That was at least hopeful. She was greatly relieved and her unexplained fear left her there and then. But that was not the end of it. At home she told her mother. Now her mother was the director of a big factory and a very resolute lady indeed. Moreover she was friendly with the superintendent of police. Straightaway she rang this worthy official and filed a complaint. The police visited "Uncle John", searched his house and found a little black book full of girls' names.

They confiscated this book and showed it to me as, of course, I was involved in this case right from the start. A slight complication was that "Uncle John" was also one of my patients. He had even given lessons to my eldest son who, after he was already thirty, told me, "I hated that man."

In the little black book one name struck me. It was another 16-year-old girl in my practice. I shall call her Kitty.

I had always liked Kitty. She was a rather shy, awkward girl and she was in the habit of visiting me every time she had a good report from her school and moved to a higher class.

Looking back on this habit of hers, I can now see that it was a cry for help, which I did not recognise.

I went to her house and spoke to her alone and then, to my dismay, discovered that "Uncle John" had sexually abused her from her twelfth year onwards. Kitty, contrary to the first girl, was severely damaged.

Uncle John was put on trial and was very angry with me indeed. I even felt a little bit guilty about having had to do this to a patient, but then I learnt that, during the war, he had been an SS man. At that moment my guilt vanished like snow in summer.

The two girls were key witnesses at the trial and Uncle John disappeared behind bars for the appropriate time of 9 months.

But then something peculiar happened. Kitty felt guilty about having done this to Uncle John, who had also been an intimate friend of her family. It was her testimony that had finally clinched the matter. She was free from him and that was a relief, but she was the one who had put him in prison and this weighed heavily on her conscience.

I had a long talk with her but to no avail.

At one moment I said, "Listen, all this is part of a greater whole. Your experience, his going to prison, it all belongs together. It is not you who had put him there, it was already part of the general pattern that was going to unfold. Your role is in fact a minor one."

"I do not believe you," she answered.

"Don't you believe that everything is united in a greater whole?" I asked.

"No, not at all. Why should it be?"

"Well, the Chinese would not agree with you. They would say that you and I, sitting here, and Uncle John in prison, and the trial all belong together and they could even prove those things with the *I Ching*, a book of wisdom."

I took the book from the bookshelf and also fifty small milfoil stems, another means of arriving at the right hexagram. More or less to amuse her and to take her mind off Uncle John I threw the milfoil stems and showed her how I built up a hexagram.

All this happened thirty years ago and I have to produce the right hexagram from memory, but I am nearly certain it was No. 29, "The Unfathomable". I believe my memory is right because there is hardly any other one that mentions the thing I am now going to describe.

Look at the commentaries: "By repeating the danger one gets used to it."

This of course could have been applied directly to her abuse which

47

had lasted for many years. But most revealing was the commentary given with the sixth line (which in the case of this hexagram was a six and so had to be consulted): "A man, who in great danger has erred from the right way and has been hopelessly entangled in his sins without any prospect of getting out of the situation. He is like a criminal, who sits in prison, surrounded by thorns, with manacled hands."

"Did you know this beforehand?" she asked me a little bit suspiciously.

"No, it comes as a complete surprise to me."

It was for her a mind-boggling experience. How was such a thing possible? Hadn't all these things happened by chance?

Suddenly she caught a glimpse of that great pattern of which she was only a tiny part and it helped her. Yes, she had played a role in Uncle John's imprisonment, but she had not put him there and she was ordained to play this role, though at the time she had not realised it.

By the way, one should not take the *I Ching* commentary too literally. Manacled hands and thorns are a thing of the past. In Dutch prisons, it's more usual to find TV and sports.

Kitty had a long road to travel before she was cured of her past, but cured she was, and she made a happy marriage, became the mother of beautiful children and even qualified as a medical doctor who helped many people.

It was the only time in my life I ever cast from the *I Ching* for a patient and I had beginners' luck.

It was one of those moments in my life when I realised how utterly strange this existence is. I haven't even started to understand it yet.

SOMEHOW COINCIDENCES ARE attracted by books.

Is it that everything creative must be related to the mysterious realm where coincidences spring from?

Sometimes it is just a little thing, a smile from heaven, one could say.

On 10 January 1990 I received a telephone call from Karin, an actress and a former patient, who was now living in the middle of Holland. I had not seen her or spoken to her for many years.

She wanted to know the exact title of a rare book I had once shown her in the past. It was full of astrological pictures. It was the book I mentioned in the chapter about astrology. The exact title is *Les 360 Degrés du Zodiac symbolisés par l'Image et par la Cabale*, written by Janduz (J. Duzéa) and published in Paris in 1938.

It was then absolutely impossible to obtain a copy, not even from a good antiquarian, and most people, astrologers included, did not know it existed. Strangely enough, the Koppejan reprint came out that same year, but I did not know that at the time. I regretfully had to inform her, after having given her the title, that she would look for it in vain.

Exactly ten minutes later one of my patients during consulting hour asked me the same question: "What was the exact title of that book with all the interesting pictures?"

Now one could say, "Big deal. You obviously show that book to many patients. Is it to be wondered at that they now and then ask for the title?"

Then I must inform such a person that I hardly ever show a patient pictures, and have certainly not done so during the last 20 years. I received the book from my astrological teacher, that same Koppejan, in March 1954 and in the 36 years since then, I had only once before, long ago, had this request. This boils down to three patients in 36 years with two in quick succession, while one of them had been out of my range of sight for many years.

What with the rareness of the book and the unfamiliarity of the general public with its existence, I am entitled to give the occurrence a place in this book.

The phenomenon likes to give you little nudges, jolts, and answers to simple questions as if to say, "Don't forget, I am here."

Those who have read a lot will probably have experienced coincidences like the ones described below.

On 30 October 1990 I was reading a book by C. S. Lewis and in it he mentioned Boswell's *Johnson*, as if it were a book well known to every civilised person and needing no further explanation.

I felt extremely uncivilised as I had never hear of it and it kept nagging at my mind. So on 2 November during a spare moment rather late in the morning, I decided to remedy my cultural ignorance and look Boswell up in the encyclopaedia. Indeed, there he was and Johnson too.

Early that afternoon An, my wife, came back from the public library. I asked her if she had found a nice book and she showed it to me – *The Private Life of Dr Watson*. I have forgotten the name of the writer. I opened it and there on the first page I read: "I am lost without my Boswell," followed by a quotation from Dr Samuel Johnson.

My wife, by the way, had not been aware of the dent made in my vanity by C. S. Lewis' remark and how it had rankled in me for a couple of days. Incidentally, if the reader is an odd man out and has never heard of Boswell, either, let me give him a few details.

James Boswell, born in 1740, was – as everyone knows – a member of a literary club founded by Johnson and he wrote Johnson's biography, *Life of S. Johnson*, in 1791. It was published in London.

I have already told the story about the double-agent King Kong and the coincidence of a colleague visiting me just at the right moment to unleash a real cascade of events.

This, however, was not the only coincidence connected with my book *Science Knows No Tears*. There was a second one but I have to lead up to it with the description of an impressive movie I saw long ago.

I often use the story from that film in my practice to help people when they despondently say,, "There is no sense in my life. Why am I here?"

So please bear with me for a moment and listen to the contents of that movie. I do not quite remember who was playing the leading part. Was it James Stewart or Gregory Peck? In any case, it was one of those likeable film stars from the many movies we saw soon after the war, when we in the liberated countries caught up with famous English and American films.

The movie was about a nice man who fell into a mid-life crisis. He lived in a town on the banks of a large river. It was a beautiful town, well run, clean, prosperous, full of friendly people, and it possessed a port with many ships going in and out.

This man, in his depression one misty evening in the autumn, walks away from home, roams the streets and finally arrives at the bridge spanning the river. By now his mood is so black that he decides to end it all. He climbs the railing and is about to jump into the river (cut to dark water swirling ominously under the bridge).

Just before he jumps, however, another man suddenly appears and asks him, "Whatever are you doing?"

"Is that any of your business?" the jumper asks him bitterly.

"Well, yes, in a sense it is, you know. Tell me about it."

Then this man, about to commit suicide, tells the story I hear in my office time and time again, if not in quite the same words: "My life makes no sense. I have never done anything of importance. My wife could have found a better husband, my children a better father. Anyone could do in my profession what I have done."

At least that it how I recall the film.

"Well," says the little man who has interrupted the depressive one, "if that is your problem something can perhaps be arranged. I am an angel of God, you know, and you are my first assignment. If I make a good job of it I might even be promoted."

Now this is going too far for the poor man on the railing and he jumps.

There is one slight miscalculation in his plan. He can swim very well and moreover the angel – for it is a real one – jumps with him.

Wet through, they swim to the shore and soon, wrapped in warm blankets, they sit in the lock-keeper's warm room, drinking hot coffee.

"Well, how about it?" the angel asks his companion.

The black mood has not left Gregory or James or whoever played the role. Also he is frustrated now because there he is, not bright but certainly alive and kicking.

The man looks at the angel and says, "I wish I had never lived."

"Rather a tough proposition that, I must consult someone higher up," the angel says, but in the blink of an eye he appears to have been in contact with his superiors for he says, "It is all arranged. You have never lived," and vanishes.

The depressed man's curiosity has been tickled, which is a good remedy against gloom, and, forgetting his suicidal plans, he puts on his suit that by now had been dried by the fire, takes his leave of the lock-keeper and walks back into town. A big surprise awaits him. It has become another town overnight.

In the harbour rusty ships, some half under water, lie idle. The area has become a dangerous neighbourhood, full of prostitutes and drunken men. The farther he proceeds, the more astonished he becomes. Not one house is the same as he remembers it. The town seems completely dilapidated. Criminality is rampant. No one is friendly any more. In his usual pub there are fights, people snarl at each other.

In the public library he finds his wife, a rather batty spinster, who yells with fright when he embraces her, and calls the police.

He now tries to discover what has happened and slowly retraces the steps of a life that has never been. He finds out that all the many seemingly unimportant small actions, which every person performs in his or her life thousands of times, have added up to a sum total, which means the difference between a good town and a bad one.

He finds, for instance, that as a child he has just prevented his younger brother from stepping in front of an oncoming truck. Now – because he has not lived – he finds the grave of this child, while the brother, when alive as a grown-up man, had been the founder of the agricultural loan bank, which brought prosperity to many people who otherwise would have remained poor.

At another time his vote had secured the election of a man to the Town Council who was to be a great stimulant to the cultural life of the town. Had his political opponent been elected, it would have been an unmitigated disaster.

And so it continues, one small event after another.

Of course, at the end, he runs back to the bridge, begs the angel who is waiting for him to give him back his life, the request is granted and he returns to his same old life, but no longer is it dull. Every moment is filled with meaning.

When it is written in the Bible that the old patriarchs died – as, for instance, is said of Abraham (Genesis 25:8) "full of years" – the Hebrew word for "full" is "satisfied". What is meant is that they had learned in their long lives to fill every moment with meaning.

The angel, having done a good job, was promoted.

When I tell this story in my office, I always pause at this moment, letting it sink in, and then I say, "You are that man [or that woman, though it is more often the male patients who need it]. You and I are part of a community, a greater and mainly invisible whole, and when we lead a decent life, nothing spectacular, just doing what we have to do, everyone of us is like that man in the film, and without us the whole town would fall apart."

Thus the story has become an antidote against that terrible illness of our 20th century – the feeling that life has no meaning. It is *the* catastrophic epidemic of our time. In many seriously ill patients the feeling of significance has first to be restored before a real cure can be expected.

What has this film to do with coincidence?

In *Science Knows No Tears*, published in 1980, I used this story on page 149 to illustrate the point that everyone as long as he or she lives is irreplaceable, essential in the great pattern of life. I stress the fact that the importance of the things we do is often hidden from us, but that all of us are needed.

In January 1981 I received a telephone call from a colleague, a general practitioner in my home town, and he told me the following story.

He had been reading my book, sitting upstairs in his study. When he had finished the story of the depressed man, he shut the book and walked downstairs, where his wife was watching TV in the sitting-room. An old film was being repeated and he caught the last ten minutes of it. Yes, of course, it was the film I have just described.

Sometimes the phenomenon just pokes fun at you. On 7 September 1992 I opened a book from the public library and there I found an invitation to a surprise party. It was to celebrate the wedding anniversary of people I did not know. A telephone number was given for those who wanted to confirm that they were able to come.

Fearing that someone had lost this invitation and so would miss a pleasant evening, I called the number.

Now one must realise that I live in the midst of 250,000 people, most of them unknown to me. Yet the voice that answered me was somehow familiar. I gave my name and the woman at the other end of the line asked, "Why, doc, what a nice surprise. What can I do for you?" Then I recognized the voice. It was a woman I had had in my practice for many years and who was still under supervision.

We were astonished that I had picked just that book from among the tens of thousands in the public library, in which her telephone number had been written on a forgotten invitation, and that I, out of the 250,000 people in this region, should have been the one to find it. It was far beyond normal chance.

I did not go to the surprise party.

These, as you can see, are all small and yet significant stories, just the sort of coincidences that happen to everyone now and again. They remind us of the invisible web we are moving and living in. Here is another one.

On Sunday afternoon, 29 January 1984, I was reading the book

Scarlet Night by Dorothy Salisbury David. On page 149 she wrote something about the *Book of Kelts*, an ancient Irish manuscript unknown to me. I had just finished this passage when Emily, my assistant, dropped in. She had just returned from Amsterdam and told us she had visited the Irish expedition and that one of the most beautiful things she had seen was the *Book of Kelts*. She had even bought four picture postcards of it, which she showed us. So now I knew what the *Book of Kelts* was.

AS CHANCE
WOULD HAVE IT

I am an adviser to two publishing firms on the subject of medical books. When they receive a manuscript from a writer or a medical book published in English, French or German, they sometimes ask me to evaluate it for them: is it something for our country or not? Sometimes (very seldom) it is the other way round and I point out a particularly important book to them.

On rare occasions I have to do more. They ask me to edit the book for the Dutch market and even, once in a blue moon, I am asked to write the foreword.

Early in 1992 the publishing firm INTRO (one of the two) asked me to edit the book *Getting Well Again* by Carl and Stephanie Simonton and James Creighton and also to write a foreword to the Dutch edition. Two rare requests rolled into one.

Carl is a radiologist from Texas who got rather depressed because so many of his cancer patients eventually died. He discussed this with Stephanie (at least this is how I heard the story), his wife, who is a psychologist. She encouraged him to use psychological methods together with the orthodox therapy.

They were much influenced by the important work done by one of the great pioneers in psychological treatment of cancer, Lawrence Leshan, whose first book on the subject was *You Can Fight for Your Life*.

I knew both the Simontons and undertook the task gladly. The book became a great success in the Dutch market, and, by 1977, had been reprinted 9 times.

Late in 1991 I advised the other publishing firm, Ankh Hermes (on my own initiative), to have the book *Vaccination and Immunisation* by Leon Chaitow translated.

A short explanation is called for.

Babies have an incompletely developed immune system, certainly until the 9th month. Professor Gorter, my medical mentor in the children's ward of the Academic Hospital in Leyden, always said that one should never give a child under 9 months vaccinations.

Yet the medical authorities in Holland, in their superior wisdom, give all babies the following vaccinations, with mitigated or killed bacterial and viral solutions, to which certain other non-physiological substances have been added for sterilisation purposes.

Month 3   DWTP (diphtheria, whooping cough, tetanus and polio-
            myelitis) + Hib (haemophilus influenza b)
Month 4   DWTP + Hib
Month 5   DWTP + Hib
Month 14   DWTP + MMR (mumps, measles, rubella)

Mind you, this is a completely unphysiological procedure. In the first place children seldom had their children's diseases before they became toddlers; and in the second place they never got them all at the same time; and in the third place these diseases are fought by the immune system at the skin and mucus layers, while the injection places the confrontation directly in the blood, the second line of defence.

Even a dimwit can understand that this scheme must give trouble, and trouble there is, in plenty, though no medical official is ready to admit it.

We are lucky that in homoeopathic circles an excellent procedure has been found to neutralise or at least mitigate the alarming side-effects. One doctor in particular, Tinus Smits, has discovered a cure with a very effective series of completely innocent homoeopathic remedies, so-called "nosodes".

Apparently his exploits, with their really amazing results, are beginning to cause anxiety in the minds of those in power. If one has success in curing the many victims of vaccinations, then these victims must be there. So these medical authorities have recently cooked up a new idea: nosodes are to be prohibited in the Netherlands.

When children may no longer be cured with a remedy which proves that their alarming symptoms came from their vaccinations, then one has turned off the light and can deny that vaccinations were the culprits.

However, this book is not about vaccinations. I only wanted to make clear why I went out of my way to recommend Leon Chaitow's book, which describes many side-effects and many flaws in the whole philosophy behind mass vaccination. The book is a real whistle-blower and deflates the jubilant stories about the miraculous results achieved through vaccinations. Chaitow places himself in line with the little street urchin in Andersen's fairy-tale "The Emperor's New Clothes" who cried that the emperor hadn't got anything on. This fairy-tale, by the way, is one of the greatest prophecies ever made about the 20th century.

Ankh Hermes followed my advice and even asked me to edit the book and write a foreword, another double-helping of rare occurrence.

Let me repeat: occasionally I read a book for one or two publishing firms. Not often. On extremely rare occasions I edit a book I have recommended. Most of my spare time is taken up with my practice, and I am not an official editor. On even rarer occasions I am asked to write a foreword.

Now let us look at what happened.

On 30 September 1992 I received proofs from Ankh Hermes of Chaitow's book, the one I had edited and provided with a foreword.

On 1 October 1992 I received from Intro proofs of the book written by the Simontons, which I had both edited and provided with a foreword.

How much coincidence is involved here I cannot possibly calculate, but the amount must be simply enormous, given how many people are engaged in preparing proofs and bearing in mind how extremely rare the combination of editing and writing forewords is for me. To receive the two sets of proofs on two successive days is really something to commemorate.

The next story is a rather sad one.

In 1980 I had a patient called Els. She was 17 years old and she was in the last stages of a malignant tumour.

On 1 February 1980, when she was very weak, she received a visit from her entire dancing club. One of the boys had a bad stutter.

Now, as it happens, in the Netherlands we had a popular writer of teenager books, called Top Naeff. One of her books is called *School Idylls* and it describes the life of a 17-year-old girl. She falls ill with tuberculosis, as was the case with so many young people at the beginning of the century, and she lies dying at home (just like Els). Then her entire dancing club comes to visit her shortly before her death and among the boys one has a bad stutter.

On that day of the visit Els was already so far gone that she could hardly speak, but – as her mother told me afterwards – when her friends had left she whispered to her, "School Idylls."

She had recognised the pattern.

On 6 February she became so ill that the ambulance was called to take her to hospital. At the moment it arrived she died at 7.30 p.m.

Is this a real example of a coincidence? Yes, I certainly think so and for 4 reasons:–

Firstly: they were not just boys and girls but it was her dancing club.

Secondly: there was a boy with a bad stutter among the friends.

Thirdly: Els was 17.

Fourthly: it was a few days before her death.

All four factors in the book *School Idylls* had been given real counterparts.

I am aware of the fact that today many young women die also, though not from tuberculosis any more, but because they have been on the contraceptive pill from a very young age and are thus more prone to develop cancer. (viciously denied by the authorities but absolutely proven by Ellen Grant in her books *The Bitter Pill* and *Sexual Chemistry*. By the way, Els was not on the pill.)

But the circumstances of the dancing club's visit are too similar to those in the book to merit any other description than that of a striking coincidence.

Moreover there is the undeniable fact that Els recognised the meaningful connection and thought it so important that she struggled to tell her mother.

Two of the most astonishing coincidences connected with books I have saved for the last part of this chapter.

Before telling these stories, however, I shall have to sketch in the background.

In February 1988 a young woman, aged nearly 22, called Mara (not her real name), living approximately 20 miles south of Haarlem, visited me, accompanied by her parents. She was having difficulty walking. She was suffering from a progressive paralysis of all her muscles, called ALS ("Amyotrophic Lateral Sclerosis"). Within a year she was completely paralysed. She literally could not lift her little finger any more. When she could no longer visit me, I went to her house. Soon the muscles in her thorax began to fail and the surgeon had to put a tube directly into her windpipe for artificial respiration. I shall never forget the day before this operation, when she thanked me for the last time for the fact that I had tried to help her, because she knew that from the next day onward she would be unable to speak. Swallowing also became impossible and she had to be fed through a tube, entering through her nose and ending in her stomach. The only thing left to her were her eye movements and with the help of an alphabet she was able to communicate with us. Her brain remained sharp as a needle.

She was deeply attached to an older sister, who was married and had three children. This sister suddenly developed the same illness and, with the example of the younger one in her mind, she refused artificial respiration and suffocated. This was an enormous emotional shock to my patient, who now for the first time began to show signs of depression. Later it was found that the sisters had grown up in a house, where the soil was full of poison, a chemical pollutant. They were not the only ones who had suffered paralysis.

We all expected Mara to die soon, but she lived on and on.

One would expect that such a pitiable patient had enough to bear but there was another major complication in her life. The family belonged to some strict religious sect. TV, radio, cassette-recorders, and secular literature were forbidden. A human being should use every spare moment to direct his or her thoughts towards God. The only excitement was a church-service held in her house. I never witnessed such a service but my assistant told me that great emphasis was laid on the extreme sinfulness of man. In short, Mara's soul was also severely paralysed.

Verses like David's cry of joy: "When I am in trouble, you come to my relief", or Jesus saying: "My yoke is easy and My burden is light" (Psalm 4, and Matthew 11:30), had fallen on deaf ears in that sect.

Just imagine Mara's position – on her back, unable to move anything but her eyes from right to left or from left to right. Moreover, she was severely discouraged from experiencing things that give joy to most of us.

Nursing Mara was a Herculean job. Three women (male help was forbidden) had to be with her, each one for 8 hours continuously out of every 24. One of the complications was that she could not swallow and her saliva had to be sucked out mechanically every so often, because it could flow down to her lungs. Her eyes had to receive extra care as she could not close them of her own accord and they threatened to dry out.

After three years of this inconceivable physical and mental suffering Mara became dangerously depressed and she dictated to me, "I fear that I am going mad."

I felt completely helpless in this situation and had a talk about Mara with my third son, a GP just like me. He listened to the whole story with great attention and said, "What she has got is sensory deprivation."

I understood the term immediately. A chronic lack of sensory input had darkened her life beyond endurance.

We hardly realise when we are healthy how important a variety of sensory stimulations is for us. This stimulation is at least as necessary as food and drink and even air.

Mara could not stretch out her hands to feel something. She could not feel the position of her joints, a feeling we are not conscious of, but which gives us a sense of certainty as long as we are awake. Much of our feeling of self is connected with the constant knowledge of what our muscles are doing and how our joints are stretched or bent.

Mara could not smell, because she did not breathe through her nose. She could not taste because food went directly to her stomach. She could only see her own small room and as time went by not even that for, eventually, she became blind.

She could hear perfectly, but what she heard was always the same sort of conversation. One could say that, for her, there was literally nothing new under the sun.

My assistant began to write letters to her, but I had a feeling that something more was needed, so one day I described in detail the walk I made every week through the dunes, and illustrated it with photos. It was an overwhelming success and then an idea came to me. Seeing how she had lapped up my story as a hungry cat laps up milk, I decided to try and write fiction for her. A forbidden commodity, I knew, but perhaps coming from me it might slip through the censor.

Shortly after I had taken that decision, I went for a holiday in France. So, in the summer of 1992, sitting in a beautiful garden under a eucalyptus tree, I began writing a book for her.

Writing fiction proved to be sensational. Something immediately took over and every morning I awoke with the next part ready to be written down. I did not have to imagine anything, I just had to record what had arrived during the night. I now understood Tolkien better, who wrote somewhere that he saw a man sitting in the pub in Bree and asked himself who that could be. It proved to be Aragorn, as great a surprise for the writer as for his readers.

Often during the evening, I would tell my wife, "I wonder how Gadja [the heroine of the book] gets out of this one," but she always managed without my help. This made the story as exciting for me as it later proved to be for Mara and her helpers, who all looked out for it. I gave it to her in instalments of twice a week. That way she had something to look forward to.

The heroine was a young girl living at about the time of the French Revolution. She went through the most incredible adventures, escaped from the tightest corners and showed a great deal of independence and inventiveness. One of the most striking things in the story was that she entered another world, where the most dangerous

59

but also the most marvellous things happened to her. As a matter of fact the structure of the book was that of Dante's *Divine Comedy*, set in the 18th century, and she went through hell, purgatory and the first halls of heaven.

It struck me that many of her experiences in some way reflected the emotional turmoil in Mara's soul and indeed later on when she reached those passages she sometimes said, "That is exactly how I feel."

It was not only Mara and the nurses who read the weekly instalments avidly. One day Mara's father made a remark from which I gathered that he also read the book. I was rather pleased until he said, "Of course I read the book. I must control what Mara reads." She was then 26 years old. When he said "read" he meant of course that the book was read to her. It was impossible for her to read things.

Against all expectations Mara lived on and so I went on writing or, rather, "receiving" books during the summer holidays that followed.

Every time, I received enough for a whole year and every time, the book was about a young woman, who gave an example to Mara of how to think independently, how to be free, notwithstanding the fact that her body was bound or in prison, how to roam in other worlds where adventures still happened and in plenty.

In this way five books were written and the heroines of the five books were all related. The seventh child of Gadja was a girl called Dori. She lived in the 19th century and was born in Strasbourg, though later on she moved to Paris.

The daughter of Dori was Susan but there is no book about her.

Susan had twin girls called Debora and Julia, and they were born in St Malo, Brittany. Debora is the heroine of the third book.

Next in line comes Jacqueline, Debora's daughter, born in a small village in Alsace where she goes through World War One. She later moves to Amsterdam. There she goes through World War Two.

Her daughter is Claire, whose history is not related, and the final book is about Claire's daughter, Lilianne, who was born in Bloemendaal in the eighties.

Now these five books did not come in orderly procession. They happened like this: Gadja . . . Lilianne . . . Debora . . . Jacqueline . . . Dori, in the numerical sequence 1 . . . 5 . . . 3 . . . 4 . . . 2. As I write, the fifth book is still being read to Mara but this summer I did not have inspiration for a sixth one.

Instead of that this book was written. So until August Mara's mind can leave her incarceration and roam other worlds. What happens later I do not know, but perhaps she will at last have obtained the freedom to hear every book she wants.

This lengthy introduction was necessary in order to understand the remarkable coincidences connected with these books, two of them in this chapter, one of them in chapter 8, and one in chapter 12.

Debora (book 3 in both sequences) and her twin sister Julia were born in 1886. Julia is a pushy, dominant girl and Debora a rather timid, silent young woman, easily led by her sister.

One day the two sisters go for a walk on the endless beaches outside their beautiful old home town, St Malo. When they have walked for some time, Debora sits down on a boulder for a moment, while Julia walks on a few paces. Then suddenly Julia vanishes. Her footsteps in the sand can still clearly be seen, but she herself has evaporated into thin air. Debora stares, totally bewildered, at the place where her sister's footsteps have stopped. On that wide beach where there is no place for Julia to hide herself, Debora is for the first time utterly alone.

As the story unfolds Debora, with the help of an elderly, kind-hearted and also highly gifted professor, discovers that Julia has stepped into a parallel universe.

Aided by her old friend she manages to follow Julia into that other world, where everything mirrors our own world. There she finds another St Malo, another France and all the countries of our world. Only everything is quite different. Debora becomes the dominant twin and Julia becomes the victim of a cruel regime holding sway over the population of that mirror planet. There is one central totalitarian government in that world, located in a mirror Jerusalem.

Of course I am not going to summarize the contents of the book (though I hope the five books will one day be published) but in order to make the coincidence clear I must say a bit more about the book.

Julia has been taken prisoner. Debora manages to free her and they escape on a ship, sailing from the south coast of France. During a terrible storm, Debora is flung overboard and later on when the ship reaches the island of Rhodes, Julia is taken prisoner again and brought to the headquarters in Jerusalem.

Debora in the meantime has been saved and has an out-of-body experience. She is taken on a journey by a small, rather mischievous, Arab boy on a flying carpet in order to reconnoitre the headquarters of the world government in Jerusalem, where unknown to her Julia is held captive in the dungeons.

They are flying over the eastern part of the Mediterranean and nearing the coast of what we call Israel, approximately near Jaffa.

Here comes an exact quotation from that page: "Soon a coastline loomed up. She saw a tremendous surf and then they were flying inland. At first the country was rather flat with orange groves. She could clearly distinguish the bright orange colour of the fruit between the dark green of the leaves.

The journey led straight towards high, dark hills and then they shot upwards on a diagonal course until she saw a white town lying on the hills. Soon they were right above the town and their strange little airship stopped and hung still in the air.

She looked down and gave a violent start. In the middle of the town, on a high hill, lay an enormous octopus. Its oval grey body was elevated on top of the hill in a soft lump. Two big saucer-like eyes at the front of the lump stared glassily into space. Eight twisting tentacles sprouted forward from the head and in-between she could clearly distinguish the parrot-like beak.

'What is that monster, Joessoef?' she asked, thoroughly frightened.

'A monster that is holding the whole world in its grip, noble lady.'

To her horror the carpet began a rapid descent straight towards the octopus and then suddenly she saw that it was not a living animal. The grey body was a great, smooth, dome-shaped building, with as its only windows, the two glass spheres she had taken for eyes. The tentacles were oblong extensions with many small windows like port-holes, made to look like suckers. The penthouse over the entrance, together with the steps leading up to the front gate, gave the impression of a slightly opened parrot beak."

As Mara was not yet blind at the time, I illustrated this page with an aerial picture of Jerusalem, a large octopus on top, his tentacles hanging over the city.

I wrote this part of the book in June 1994 in the garden in southern France.

On 15 March 1995 this story of the octopus was read to Mara.

On 18 March an article was published in *The Telegraph*, the daily paper in the Netherlands. I will translate it here (that part relevant to our story).

Die dag daarvoor waren joodse instellingen in de residentie door bezorgde burgers algewaarschuwd voor eengruwelijke afbeelding die voor de ramen van tal van huizen van moslim-bewoners in de Schilderswijk hing: een enorme octopus die met zijn tentakels over Jeruzalem hangt. Het hoofd van het monster is een doodskop met daarin gebrand een joodse davidster.

Ronny Naftaniël van het CIDI, het Centrum Informatie en Documentatie Israël: „We hebben vele geschokte reacties gekregen. Die octopus werd op deze manier al door de nazi's gebruikt om de jodenhaat aan te wakkeren, hier is sprake van een zeer gevaarlijke ontwikkeling die moet worden gestopt. Anders vallen er straks slachtoffers."

"The previous day the Jewish authorities in the capital [Jerusalem] were warned by apprehensive citizens about an atrocious picture hanging behind the windows of many houses inhabited by Moslems in the Painters' Quarter which depicts an enormous octopus hanging with its tentacles over Jerusalem."

(*Up to here the coincidence is uncannily accurate*)

"The head of the monster is a skull with the Jewish star of David burned into it."

Here the similarity seems to stop, but that is not the case. Later on Debora discovers something that makes the similarity even more precise.

When at last she manages to enter the building, she finds that the whole impressive headquarters is no more than an empty shell, devoid of any suggested mystical meaning. An elaborate hoax to hoodwink the world. There is no secret power at all within the building, it is no more than an empty skull. When the exterior similarity stops, symbolic similarity takes over and only the star of David has no place in my book.

The article concludes: "Ronny Naftaniël of the CIDI, the Centre for Information and Documentation in Israel, says: 'Many reports of upset reactions have been received. This octopus was used in such a manner once before by the Nazis to inflame hatred against the Jews. This is a very dangerous development that has to be stopped because otherwise people will get hurt'".

The picture was probably used in Germany, we never saw it in the Netherlands. But the last sentence again applies directly to the story of Debora. She absolutely has to put a stop to the operations of the octopus, as her sister and the man she has fallen in love with have been brought there, to be slowly killed in the dungeons.

The weekly readings to Mara about young women who courageously maintained their integrity under overwhelming physical and moral pressure and under no circumstances could be intimidated, however much their enemies tried, after five years suddenly began to take effect. At least that is how I interpreted the situation which then developed.

In 1997, Mara was 31 years old, and she rebelled against her father. She told her mother to buy a cassette-recorder and paid for this with her own money.

So when I visited her on Wednesday 2 April and entered her room, the heavenly music of Beethoven's violin concerto floated towards me. She had chosen a really dramatic moment for this dénouement. Her father, who as always had followed me to her room, was suddenly confronted with this shattering of the taboo and received a severe shock. He had not been aware of this new development. Her mother, unwilling to face the consequences, fled downstairs. Her father was white with rage but, as I was there, he repressed his feelings, while I praised the beautiful music. But as soon as I left, he straightaway confiscated the new recorder and took it back to the shop. His subsequent behaviour was even more terrible. There was a warning that he might interfere with the air supply if Mara didn't obey him.

Mara tried to make it clear that she wanted the freedom to choose her own books and her own music, and even her own privacy as far as possible, but to no avail.

I have never in my 44 years as a medical doctor witnessed a spiritual terrorisation like that.

After the cassette-recorder incident, control, already tight, increased. An instructive book from a Jewish writer, a present from one of her helpers, was declared Satanic and forbidden.

I witnessed a scene where he openly, though in carefully-chosen words, threatened her, his completely dependent and totally paralysed daughter. Since the war I have never come so close to attacking someone physically.

My position was a difficult one. She did not live in my home town but in the region where all the bulbs are cultivated. I was not her official GP and was only allowed to visit her with the permission of that GP. I was, to put it in formal terms, just a guest.

But Mara, having tasted freedom for the first time in her life, fought back with all the moral strength she could muster. The movement of her eyes had by now nearly stopped and it was difficult to communicate with her, but with her remaining strength she resisted the impossible pressure.

The reader might get the wrong impression that I was the helper in the battle. I was not. The real tower of strength for Mara was someone else. I will you about her presently.

First, however, the coincidence.

After the confrontation on 2 April 1997, weeks of bickering with the father followed, escalating in May to a new climax when Mara put her (spiritual) foot down and, to my utter astonishment, a new cassette-recorder appeared. It was, however, a Pyrrhic victory, for during most of the day the cassette-recorder had to be kept under lock and key, in case other members of the sect might pay a visit to Mara and see the offending machine.

It was during this time that the book about Dori was read to Mara.

As I have already mentioned, Dori lived in Strasbourg (in the 19th century), where her father was the well-known minister of a Protestant church. Of course she also got involved in the most impossible and dangerous situations. She had to fight against a secret organisation striving for world power, called the Illuminati (this conspiracy was a historical fact), and thanks to a certain inborn clairvoyant gift, she becomes so dangerous to her enemies, that they decide to do something about her.

They do not plan simply to eliminate her, but they want to enslave her in an occult way and so make her powers work for them. To this end, they make use of an expert in black magic, a Tibetan monk called Tan Po. This man has the power to drive people from their bodies and use their souls on the other side as his slaves, but he can only do so as long as he holds their bodies captive.

Now I must interrupt this story a moment and return to Mara.

On 23 April 1997 the new cassette-recorder appeared in Mara's room, playing, to my bewilderment, not Beethoven but pop music.

On 7 May the bomb went off and the new recorder had to stay in the cupboard most of the time. The father also decreed that from now on everything read to her should first pass his censorship. (Up till then, from time to time, the odd thing had slipped through, apparently.)

Those of the nursing staff, who did not want to comply with the rules, were given to understand that in that case they had to leave.

I completely blew my top, and called him every name in my vocabulary, and stamped out of the house, frothing at the mouth. Mara's father had apparently decided to batter her into submission once and for all.

And again Mara prevailed. How it happened I do not know but her father took a step back. Only a small step, it is true, but it was a beginning. During the week when Mara prevailed over her father, six pages of the book *Dori* were read to her. I had written them exactly one year earlier in May 1996 when I had no inkling of the impending crisis.

So here we have Mara, going through that terrible crisis with the spiritual dictatorship she had submitted herself to all those years, and here we have the nurses reading to her part of *Dori*. Mara in her nearly hopeless struggle for a bit of individual freedom – and Dori? She had been captured by her enemies and brought to a lonely house on the border of a windswept grey lake in the northern part of the Netherlands. There, on Christmas Eve, we find her imprisoned in an icy-cold room with barred windows.

Here is what Mara heard:

"The darkness increased and the cold penetrated right through her mantle. A key grated in the lock and someone came in. She turned round and her heart skipped a beat. Before her stood the sinister Tibetan she had seen before on the island of Samos. In his right hand he carried a small oil-lamp and in his left something wrapped in a blanket. He was dressed from collar to feet in a closely fitting violet garment. He remained as still as a statue and stared at her with penetrating eyes.

'I am your teacher,' he finally said. His voice was calm and melodious. Dori shrugged her shoulders.

'You would do better to co-operate with me. I can deprive you of food and drink. I can take away your clothes, with the room remaining as cold as it now is, and I can do far more unpleasant things to you. Co-operate with me and you will get a stove, you will be fed well and you will undergo no pain or other horrors. You will even go through very interesting and educational experiences.'

'Tell me,' said Dori, 'which country are you from?'

'From Tibet.'

'You have been trained there?'

'Yes.'

'Did your teachers train you to chase people against their will out of their bodies?'

(Tan Po had done this to his prisoners in Samos with the help of a magic gong, a small model of which he held now concealed in his left hand.)

'In fact,' Dori continued, 'did your masters teach you to use other people for your own ends?'

'I do not have a master any more. I am my own master.'

He looked at her with disdain.

[Mara's father, though begged by several people to stop his reign of terror, had haughtily answered that he took his own counsel.]

'In that case you are not a real man of wisdom, for a real man of wisdom is defined as the pupil of another wise man.'

Dori had read this statement somewhere in a book lent to her by Leon, a Jewish friend.

'Sometimes a pupil can surpass his teachers and seek his own way. I am a master, *the* master, one could say.'

'If that is true you will have to obey one universal law, to wit, the law that you must leave another person alone, until that person of her own free will chooses you as her teacher.'

'Woman, you are drivelling.' He said it formally but there was rage in his eyes.

[Mara's father outwardly always remained the perfect gentleman, coming from an upper-middle-class family.]

She knew that she had managed to dent his imperturbability.

'What is your name?' she mused. 'Ah, yes, Tan Po. As you behave very insultingly towards me, I will call you just Po. In my language it is an object under the bed, a receiver of excretions. Just as you yourself are an excrement of your people. You are a scoundrel, a piece of Tibetan junk. You should be ashamed of yourself.'

[Even this speech of Dori's tallied with reality. During the bitter fight with her father Mara dictated a letter to her nurse for him using words that even I hardly knew.]

Po took a step towards her, put his oil-lamp on the floor and slapped her face so hard that she tumbled backwards onto the bed, but she got up immediately and said,

'He who uses violence to make his point has left the path of wisdom.'

For a moment she saw uncertainty in his eyes. Then he laughed.

'Clichés. I don't traffic in phrases, certainly not in hollow ones. I am the lord of reality. I will meet you on the other side and there you will not be able to oppose my will. You will not be an insolent there, but submissive, and you will obey me. I will knead you like a potter his clay.' "

Let the reader rest assured that Dori is saved from that situation. It is uncanny how this passage from *Dori* foreshadows the situation that developed a year after it was written. When I wrote about Po I was unaware of any similarity with Mara's father. I had certainly not used him as a model for Po but model he was, as I could see for myself.

Summarizing the coincidence:

In May 1996 I described a confrontation between Dori and Po that nearly exactly matched the confrontation between Mara and her father in May 1997. Moreover this passage was read to Mara precisely during that crucial week when the crisis had reached its peak.

I am convinced that the hearing of this exchange between Dori and Po gave her just that extra stamina she needed at that particular moment, but I must at the same time put this statement in context.

Mara's greatest help was a black nurse, who intuitively felt exactly what Mara felt and finally succeeded where I had failed all those years: she undammed Mara's emotions.

She did this in all sorts of ways. Sometimes she took Mara's hand, sang, and swayed the hand to and fro rhythmically. "We're dancing," she said. Another time she arranged a visit from an Irish folk singer (which Mara's father with all his might tried to prevent), and she invited along a trio to play classical music but first and foremost, she helped Mara to express her true feelings for the first time in her life. Mara's father hated and feared this nurse and called her a pernicious influence, suggesting to Mara feelings she never had. He tried to enlist my support in his struggle against that black nurse.

"She only makes Mara negative. My daughter is not like that," he complained.

This small, humble, warm, black nurse is one of the really great people I have met in my life.

Is Mara's father evil? That he acts in an evil way is beyond doubt but does he belong to those people who are bad at heart?

Scott Peck, in his book *The People of the Lie* maintains that there do exist people who are really evil and of course in ancient cultures they are described time and again. Yet I do not believe he is such a person. Rather, a thoroughly deluded one. He believes that, by acting as he does, he serves his God according to his peculiar conception of Christianity.

As a matter of fact I am grateful for the possibility he gave me of studying him at close quarters. Thanks to him I at last understood something of the thinking behind the Inquisition. I am descended from a Huguenot family and those who murdered this group of Protestants, and believed that they were doing God's work, have always interested me.

One must of course make allowances for these parents, who for 9 years had to organise their whole life around this completely paralysed daughter. The father even had to give up a lucrative job in the Hague because he was constantly needed at home. They were never free from the everlasting tension and I have compassion for them and believe that they themselves were victims of a situation that physically was perhaps just within their capabilities, but which, spiritually and morally, was far beyond them. I say "they", for the mother does not dare to stand up to her husband and protect her daughter against his spiritual terrorisation, a thing Mara knows only too well.

However these things may be, I am deeply impressed by the contrast between this self-righteous spiritual dictator and his opponent (he looks down his nose at her), that small black nurse. That invariably soft-spoken but indomitable grand lady, who helps Mara to gain maturity against all the odds.

There is a difference between Dori and Mara which I have not mentioned yet. Mara is not yet whole and of one mind. Half of her still yields to the terror, wants to co-operate, wants to shut her eyes to what is happening. Dori is, on the other hand, a sturdy lass, totally trustworthy. She is the ideal held up before Mara's eyes as a model.

I have a feeling that Mara does not die because she has to be cured of that split in her personality. I often call it "a pact with the devil". The more I think about the situation, the more I believe that it is Mara's commission in life to conquer her spiritual paralysis and to become really free. If anyone can succeed in performing that miracle, it will be the little black nurse. It is remarkable that later on in the book Dori the heroine is saved from death by a black girl.

I have included these stories about Mara because they give another dimension to the phenomenon of coincidences.

In the case of Dori's story it was as if the coincidence were commanded to serve a higher aim: to liberate a 31-year-old woman from a paralysing mental straitjacket.

Only a soul that has been liberated from bondage can love God and its neighbour out of its own free will. First there must be delivery from bondage, whatever it is, and then a soul can be saved. Not the other way round. One cannot say "I am saved" and then, to prove how saved one is, take on all sorts of nonsensical burdens that God never demanded.

The other coincidence is even more enigmatic. It seems as if there exists a connection between Mara's small, personal case and world policy.

Debora has to fight a spiritual octopus, sucking dry the soul of humanity. Mara has to fight a spiritual octopus, sucking dry her potential for becoming a whole person.

These two are connected in a mysterious way with the Arab–Jewish conflict which started 3000 years ago with Isaac and Ishmael.

How is such a thing possible?

Debora's book is all about a world mirroring our own. Are the two conflicts, one on a personal level, the other on a global scale, mirroring each other?

What is this octopus over Jerusalem? I realise that both the Nazis and the Arabs used the picture against the Jews, which is criminal, but isn't there a grain of truth in the picture itself? Are we confronted with the way in which we have betrayed our Judaeo-Christian, Bible-oriented, civilisation by leading a completely materialistic way of life, reducing God and the Saviour to mere folklore?

Haven't we, civilisation as a whole, made a pact with the devil? Haven't we wilfully gone into bondage and become spiritually paralysed? Isn't our whole civilisation prone to believe all sorts of nonsensical things?

And could this perhaps be mirroring Mara's case, or might not the two cases be of one kind? Look at Mara, in whom the joy and freedom of Christianity have been converted into pure slavery. Is that perhaps the reason why a descendant of the black slaves is teaching her to liberate herself, better than I could ever do? Isn't it all a question of bondage and how to break free?

I sincerely hope that when Mara has learned the lesson of bondage and freedom, she will be allowed to return to her heavenly Father who – I am convinced of it – will receive her with lots and lots of music.

IN THE LAST CHAPTER we have seen that there can sometimes be an element of prophecy in coincidences.

Of course humanity has tried to harness this aspect too and one of the techniques used has been the Tarot. This is a pity because the Tarot is very interesting. Prophecy has to be spontaneous and it usually turns against you when you try to force it. Originally, as we shall see, prophecy was not the aim of the Tarot.

As an introduction to the subject let me describe the following case.

On 7 July 1959 a 13-year-old boy was presented to me by his parents. He was suffering from the first stage of muscular dystrophy (Duchenne muscular dystrophy). The power in his shoulders and arms had already diminished and the muscles in his shoulders were swollen. Moreover his neurologist had confirmed the diagnosis after finding the typical metabolite in the boy's urine which is conclusive in these cases.

There exists no known cure for this illness and these children usually end up in a wheelchair before reaching adulthood.

I told the parents that I wanted to think about his case and so, on a Saturday afternoon, my first moment of leisure, I sat back and thought. Slowly before my mind's eye I paraded the symptoms of this illness and remembered a peculiar feature. At a later stage these children undergo a strange facial change (caused by flabby muscles) giving them what, I believe, Duchenne called "le museau de tapir", the "tapir's snout", with swollen cheeks and slack, pouting lips.

I now proceeded in an absolutely non-scientific way. What made a human being look like a tapir? Had he become related to a tapir? What did I know about that animal? Nothing at all.

I looked it up in Brehm's book about every animal in the world and read about the tapir. One of the things I discovered was that his diet consisted nearly exclusively of coco-palm. This was peculiar. I thought about the palm. Was it not the exact opposite of this illness? The straight, supple stem rising high up and even able to survive hurricanes.

Take a dystrophic child. He sits on the floor and cannot get up. Pitifully he tries to "climb up against himself" as the handbook calls his frantic movements.

Could this tree perhaps infuse its upright, supple and strong image into my patient? But how could that be done?

I remembered that people who eat lots of pork could often be recognised by the fat deposits in their necks and around their eyes, giving them a piggish look. Could it be that if I fed this boy coconuts, I would be able to build a palm tree into him?

7

3rd Intermezzo

Tarot

I rang his parents and suggested a diet without any animal proteins, but with lots of coconuts, including coconut-milk. Shipwrecked sailors had survived indefinitely on a coconut regime, so there was no harm in trying, and nothing to lose.

I believe this child ate a cellar-full of coconuts, the parents being very sporting people who were willing to give my crazy idea a chance.

After eighteen months the boy was completely healed, to my utter astonishment. Even the offending metabolite had vanished from his urine. His specialist was extremely annoyed with me.

This boy is now a middle-aged man himself, with a healthy son, and he has never had a relapse, though he is off coconuts.

But there is a snag in the story. Though from time to time I saw more children with muscular dystrophy, I could never repeat this performance. Was it because only the parents of that child kept religiously to his strange diet, or was it because the laws of association work just like those of coincidences – only once in the same manner?

In "Allo, Allo"* Michelle always says, "Listen carefully, I will say this only once!"

The phenomenon of coincidences and the way associations work cannot be studied according to scientific procedure. They are always unique, just like human beings. This also means that they cannot be put into statistics or controlled with double-blind tests. Scientifically speaking they are worthless. So was (in a scientific way) the curing of this boy worthless, though science has another word for it. They call it with disdain "anecdotal". A mere story, though the boy of course was glad that this story had chosen him as its hero.

What had happened? I had committed one of the capital crimes against my profession and dreamt up a therapy, instead of acting in a cold, logical and approved scientific way. I had given myself up to associative thinking, which is only permitted in psycho-analysis under strict supervision. In acting like that, I had enhanced the creative process and been given an original solution for a seemingly insoluble problem, but had also behaved like an irresponsible doctor.

Associative thinking nowadays is frowned upon as unscientific and heretical, but it has not always been considered an inferior procedure. Former civilisations had tried to encourage associative or intuitive thinking and even to enhance this process. As aids to memory they used complicated symbols that stimulated intuition rather than rationality.

* The well-known hilarious TV series about the Resistance during World War Two in France.

One of the most comprehensive symbols is that of the ten so-called "sephiroth" (hypostatized attributes by means of which the Infinite enter into relation with the finite) used in Hebrew lore. The wise men of Israel taught that creation developed in descending waves, beginning with the number 1, symbolising the Creator, and then proceeding towards the number ten, where creation ended as it symbolised our world of sensory perception. These numbers were not just placed in a descending scale like this:

1
2
3
4
5
6
7
8
9
10

but in three triangles, with one and ten at top and bottom, like this:

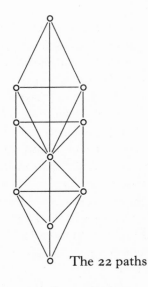

The 22 paths

Each number had a beautiful name like Kether (1), the crown, Cochmah (2), wisdom, Bina (3), understanding, Chesed (4), grace, etc. Between the ten numbers ran 22 "paths" to match the 22 letters of the Hebrew alphabet.

73

This composite symbol was said to encompass everything that existed or could possibly be conceived, both visible and invisible. It was a major help in associative thinking.

In my case with the boy who had muscular dystrophy, one could say that I had just been lucky, but this symbol provided a map into the unknown country of the spirit, increasing the likelihood – so it is said – of hitting upon deep truths, while I had merely dabbled in association.

Beginners' luck is a blessing but one cannot count on it happening again.

As it is necessary for the understanding of the Tarot, let me give an example of the insights this symbol can yield.

Number 9, Jesod or Foundation, is the invisible matrix from which our world has crystallised.

Malkhut, Kingdom, no. 10, just under 9, is our visible universe.

Rupert Sheldrake has postulated morphogenetic fields as being in existence prior to this physical world. What he talks about is Jesod in modern language. With his concept he made a severe dent in materialistic thinking, which acknowledges the physical world as the one reality and only allows the possibility of invisible emanations when they come from matter, like radioactivity or electromagnetic fields.

Sheldrake makes a valiant attempt to restore the supremacy of the invisible world over the visible one, of mind over matter, even putting mind as the original stuff of the visible world, if I have understood him well.

The invisible matrix (Jesod) of this visible world is always present and under favourable circumstances it suddenly emerges into visibility, for instance, when a thin layer of water on our windows freezes in winter and beautiful fern-like images appear.

The path between Jesod and Malkhut, between the invisible matrix and physical world, is given the last letter of the Hebrew alphabet, the Tav. This letter is associated with exile and death.

This means that, just above us, in another dimension, with possibly a higher vibration than is known to us, there exists a causative world where death does not rule supreme but everything is vibrantly alive.

Coming down into this world means going into exile, becoming mortal. The path descending from 9–10 is in essence going from life to death.

The first three chapters of Genesis stress the fact that there was no such thing as mortality in the beginning. Then something went wrong (or, rather, someone went wrong) and at a certain point death was added to an – until then – flawless creation.

In the apocryphal Book of Wisdom it says:

13: For God did not make death and has no joy in the destruction of the living.

14: For he has created all things to be and the principles of the world are wholesome and in them is no venom of destruction and the domain of hell is not on earth.

15: Righteousness is immortal. (1: 13–15)

So God did not make death. This is an important point. It *became* part of the physical realm thanks to something done by early humanity.

Ever since then, to be born in this world means to walk the road of death (Jesod to Malkhut). Dying in this world ideally would mean returning on the road towards life (Malkhut to Jesod).

It must be stated, however, that when people lead abominable lives this road is blocked and they sink even lower than Malkhut, down to a world called in that system the Klippot, the outer crusts. They have lost their inner, spiritual, lives and become totally externalised beings, like automatons. One can sometimes observe this process already happening on earth, as in the completely stereotyped mannerisms of a cruel dictator.

The letter "tav" also means "sign" and the explanation for this is that the visibility of something in the physical world demonstrates that it is a sign of having come from somewhere else, a message from a higher world. Everything in creation gives us that message.

We come from a living matrix, as does nature all around us.

An exception to this rule are those productions of the human mind which we have invented to improve on creation, like motor-cars, TV sets, computer games and space-craft.

Tagged on to the 22 paths in the composite symbol is another set of most peculiar images, called the 22 great trumps of the Tarot.

These pictures originally were probably used to help memorise the significance of each path between two sephiroth. Later on these 22 images broke loose from the composite symbol and began to lead an independent existence.

There is also a possibility that the 22 images were invented later to help in the study of the great symbol. Anyhow, they are now only loosely connected with the great composite symbol.

There exists an amusing story about how this gallery of symbols became attached to a pack of playing cards.

It is said that once, long ago, there existed an old civilisation that was drawing to its close, for both civilisations and human beings are mortal.

The wise men of that civilisation (there were of course only a few left because in a dying civilisation wisdom is nearly extinct) were saddened at the thought that so much excellent wisdom would be lost to the world and they tried to find a way to preserve the essence of what they knew.

Many plans were put forward:–

Bury it in the earth? But what about earthquakes?

Establish a secret school where wise masters entrusted the secrets to carefully selected pupils? This way the wisdom would be hidden, but not extinct, and would flourish again when better times came. But no, even wise masters have been known to become corrupt.

Carve them in imperishable stone? No, even stone gets weather-beaten in the end.

Then one of them hit upon an ingenious scheme.

He assembled the small group of wise men around him and asked them, "What is everlasting in this world? Because if we find something that is everlasting, we can entrust our wisdom to that entity."

The other men confessed that they did not know.

He smiled and said with a touch of triumph (only a touch, for he was wise), "Sin. As long as this world lasts it will be present. So let us hide our wisdom in a pack of playing cards. As long as men remain greedy, they will play for money, in pubs, in inns, on their travels, sober or drunk. And the cards will go with them. And our wisdom, hidden in the trumps, will accompany them until the time comes when wise men return to the earth and recognise what we have hidden."

That, says the legend, is the beginning of Tarot.

Some think that the cards are of Hebrew descent, pointing at the great resemblance between the word "Torah" and the word "tarot". I myself think that they were invented after Biblical times. One thing is certain: they have always had a connection with the gipsies.

Here is an example of what can be done with the great trumps. We will put to one side foretelling the future for the moment. That is a perversion of the Torah, just as killing in Christ's name is a perversion of the Bible.

The 22 great trumps of the Tarot can help us to understand more about the composite symbol.

When one looks at it, one sees that there exist three vertical rows. In the left row are three of the numbers, in the right row three, and, in the middle one, four. We will concentrate on that middle one:

1. Kether – The Crown. It is the ultimate we can understand from the Creator. In Christianity it is the Father.
6. Tipheret – Atonement. It is the centre of harmony for the whole symbol. In Christianity it is the Son.
9. Jesod Foundation – The world just around the corner. It is here that the guardian angels live.
10. Malkhut – Our World. The place of humanity.

It is extremely interesting to notice that these 4 principles are mentioned in the first verse of Revelation.

"The Revelation of JESUS CHRIST, which *God* gave unto Him, to shew unto his servants things which shortly come to pass, and He sent and signified it by His *angel* unto His servant *John*."

Let us put them in perspective:

Composite symbol, middle row	Revelation
Kether, The Father	God, the Father
Tipheret, The Son	Jesus Christ, the Son
Jesod, Place of the angels	The Angel
Malkhut, Humanity	John

One might ask, "Where is the Holy Spirit?"

In the composite symbol there is a mysterious place in another dimension. When one takes the first triangle and views it as the base of a pyramid, then the top of the pyramid is an 11th number, usually not counted in the series, called Daath, inadequately translated as "knowledge". There is a close connection with the Holy Spirit.

When Proverbs 1:7 says: "The fear of the Lord is the beginning of knowledge", this word Daath is used. It is far more than learning something in the academic sense. It is being enlightened by this primal principle, which throws light on all other things.

Now let us take a look at the paths between Kether, Tipheret, Jesod and Malkhut. They are symbolised by certain images and these images can be found in the 22 trumps of the Tarot; these paths are also numbered.

We are going to look at no. 3, between Kether and Tipheret, no. 16 between Tipheret and Jesod, and no. 22 between Jesod and Malkhut.

Here are the images belonging to the middle-paths:

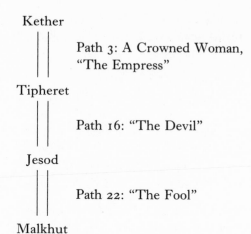

Kether

Path 3: A Crowned Woman,
"The Empress"

Tipheret

Path 16: "The Devil"

Jesod

Path 22: "The Fool"

Malkhut

Between the Father and the Son there is a crowned female. Her name is the Empress. Jesus, the son of God, was born from a woman. The Roman Catholic Church has crowned this woman as the Queen of Heaven, thus following more closely the Tarot than the Biblical text.

In the old symbol, however, something different is meant.

Every ancient tradition, Christian, Jewish or otherwise, has known that there must be a female aspect to the Godhead. One can derive this fact from the ancient text of Genesis 1:27: "And God created man in His own image, in the image of God created He him, male and female created He them."

If we are made in God's image, then the female part of God is as strong as the male part. Mind you, I am not talking about sexual differences. Sex organs belong to this earth. I am talking about the principle of there being male or female.

This is what is depicted in the 3rd path. "Do not forget the female part," it seems to say. Though of course there have been flaws in the execution, women have fared far better in the Judaeo-Christian civilisation than in any other because it never quite forgot Genesis 1:27.

Between Tipheret (The Son) and Jesod (the foundation) the Tarot places the devil. We would not have expected it. We would have expected him somewhere below Malkhut, under our feet.

The image on the composite symbol reminds us of the fact that resistance against the Saviour takes place in the heavenly realms. A real struggle is going on there, as many texts confirm.

In Daniel 10:13 a Man, who is certainly identical to the One Christians call the Son, tells Daniel that he has been hindered from coming by the "prince of the kingdom of Persia", and it is clear that a demonic entity is meant.

Paul (Ephesians 6:12) says that we do not "wrestle with blood and flesh, but with the sovereignties, with the authorities, with the world-mights of this darkness [*all fallen angels*] with the *spiritual forces of wickedness among the celestials*" (Concordant version = exact translation from the Greek).

All this ties in exactly with the place of the devil in the great graph – between the Son and the (helping) angels.

The devil, nowadays ridiculed, is portrayed in these images as a real force to be reckoned with and disquietingly high up in the heavenly realms, though firmly put under the Son.

On the path of death between Jesod and Malkhut we find the Tarot card, "The Fool".

It is the most mysterious card of all. When we think of a fool, we see someone silly in our mind's eye. That is not what is meant. This fool is different. He is not identified with the world. Letting go is his strength. The way he is drawn on the card gives us to understand that he is not a good-for-nothing, but a man who lives according to a way of life at odds with "the world". Paul says that the foolishness of God is wiser than human wisdom (1 Cor. 1:25).

It is the art of *being* in the world but not *of* the world.

It seems that two ways are open to us:–

Either we identify completely with this world and drown in it, or we do the best we can, but don't quite believe in this world.

It is apt that this "fool" belongs to the 22nd path. It is the end of the downward road and the beginning of the upward one. If a man is glued with all his senses to the physical side of existence, he may be rich and mighty, but in reality he is a fool, imprisoned on this earth. If, on the other hand, he realises his position, he becomes a pilgrim and starts to turn back to God. Then his foolishness has a divine flavour.

I believe that the Tarot was originally a help to remember the deep truths of faith. Why choose such a difficult way?

At the time when it was designed, there were no printed books, no films, no computers, nothing. Whole parts of the Bible were painted in churches, not just as decoration but as instruction. Men had to use mental aids to remember their most important insights. The best way to do this was with pictures, because they often lodge better in one's memory than words.

I believe that the Tarot was a sort of "faith encyclopaedia". Perhaps later on people began to use it in still another way. When they wanted to understand some problem in their lives, they drew a card at

random, more or less like tossing coins in the *I Ching*. If they had
formulated the question as clearly as possible, they knew that they
had tuned into the world of coincidence and stood a fair chance of
drawing the card which held the clue to their problem.

In old Jewish communities in Poland a similar thing happened. A
Jewish scholar would meditate on some part of the Torah and fail to
grasp the meaning of a word or a sentence, or some religious problem.
If he could not answer this question, he would close his books and go
off to the Jewish school. There he would wait until the children came
out and he would accost the first child he saw and ask, "Which verse
of the Torah did you have to learn by heart today?" The verse the
child had learned would invariably hold the answer to the problem
the scholar had been pondering.

What happened to the Tarot and also to astrological symbols was
sad. People began to use these gifts for their own petty purposes.
Soothsayers foretold a meeting with a handsome stranger to excited
young girls, promised a pot of gold at the end of the rainbow to
ambitious young men, and hinted of unlimited power to foolish old
men, bringing into disrepute systems that once had been used to
memorise spiritual truths.

For astrology, too, had been such a data bank. As Bullinger discovered, it started with the Virgin giving birth to a Son and ended
with the Lion conquering this evil world.

Thus the 12 signs of the zodiac originally held a great prophetic
truth and it was only much later that people began to work spells with
them.

When this degeneration started, at best, the helpful phenomenon
of coincidence would withdraw itself and not much harm was done.
The soothsayers were just liars, out for a quick buck.

But this is not always what happens. A lot of power is still left in the
old systems, and when you use them for egoistic purposes, they can
turn sour and the law of coincidence bites back with a vengeance.

Back in the thirties two young men in the Hague took a course in
astrology run by a serious teacher. When they had finished they
grinned, slapped each other on the back and, in full view of their
fellow students, cried happily, "Now for the big money!"

As a reliable witness to this event told me, they both died within six
months, one in an accident, the other from a sudden illness.

This of course is an extreme example but approaching ancient
systems connected with the phenomenon of coincidence without due
respect or with lighthearted familiarity can be disastrous, as well for
the counsellor as for the one seeking advice.

Depressions, obsessions, even demon possession can occur. One can also observe people preoccupied with these things getting hooked on their method, truly addicted. They flip completely and cannot put one foot in front of the other without consulting their particular method. I have known an astrologer who consulted the star-chart for every decision, even minor ones. A fanatical, slightly exalted, glow burns in their eyes and it is completely impossible to reason with them. They have become the slaves of a harsh master.

This is probably the main reason why the churches have warned against these systems – because they saw the victims. One should never touch a live wire with bare hands.

I personally believe as a Christian that, with the coming of Christ, all these systems became out-of-date and that, just as when the sun rises the stars vanish, these systems have lost their validity, except as interesting historical documents.

Even in Christian times they might perhaps have had some use as aids to memory during the period when there were neither books nor coloured pictures (save in churches) to remind people of the great truths of life.

We live under another dispensation nowadays, that of the Holy Ghost, who will tell us everything we need to know.

Yet it is interesting to study how the law of coincidence has been recognised throughout all the generations and how people have invented systems to activate that law, to help them through the bewildering maze of our difficult existence on earth.

I do not believe, as some Christians do, that these systems were invented by the devil to lead people astray. Originally they served as a guide in a dark world and as a help to faltering memories. I do believe, however, that they were put to wrong use and so we were perverted. It is then that the dark force, no lover of humanity, can make use of them to lead people on the road to destruction.

But this of course did not happen only to the systems we have mentioned so far.

It happened to the Christian clergy themselves, for instance, when they instigated the Inquisition and defended their action with the Bible in their hands.

It happened when priests blessed the airplanes of Mussolini, just before they took off to Abyssinia (now Ethiopia) to drop poison-gas on villages where people were still living in the Stone Age.

It happened under our very noses during the Second World War when the churches did not launch one single official protest against the Holocaust, while they knew perfectly well what was happening.

Corruption, staleness, fossilisation are hazards inherent in any human institution. That is why the study of coincidence is important. It returns a freshness, a joy, a buoyancy to life like spring after winter and rain after drought. It connects us to a source always bubbling with vitality and life.

THERE IS A certain playfulness in creation. Nowadays everything in nature is explained by scientists in the light of its evolutionary necessity and usefulness in the struggle for life, but people who talk like that are missing something essential.

Many things are there just for the fun of it.

Otters like to make a slide in the snow and there they play, sliding with the whole family and plunging with great delight into the icy-cold water.

Starlings love to imitate other birds and when one of them has done it again and I am trying to find out which kind of bird I hear, the little rascal looks at me as if it has pulled my leg on purpose.

Dogs laugh, kittens tease their mothers by clawing at the tips of their tails.

And what to think of the absurd forms we see now and then?

A monkey with a preposterous human-like nose, a baboon with his ridiculous behind, and, last but not least, the platypus, who seems to have been assembled from the junk left over when creation was finished.

Is it therefore to be wondered at that this playfulness can be found in coincidence, the phenomenon that has such a close link with original creation?

In this chapter and in the next one I will show how fun is an essential part of our subject.

NAMES

We have all come across names that for no apparent reason closely fit the profession of their bearers.

In my home town of Haarlem there was an undertaker named Kerkhof which means "Churchyard".

In my practice there was another undertaker called Rustige, which means "Quiet". This man always answered me, when I happened to meet him in summer and ask how business was going, "Quiet, Doc, all the doctors are on holiday."

For many years I thought it was just a joke, until there was a big strike by medical doctors in Los Angeles, lasting for several weeks. The overall mortality rate in the LA population plummeted dramatically, only to climb back up to its usual level when the strike was over.

Could this be the reason that a well-known GP in these regions was called Doctor de Dood? This is "Dr Death".

In one of our Haarlem hospitals there were two urologists. One of them was called Dr van Beek ("Doctor of the Brook"). The other one was called Dr de Wringer. I need not translate his name, it is the same in English.

I do not know if the patients' urine flowed more easily under the treatment of Dr van Brook compared to that of Dr de Wringer.

Then, in the same hospital, the orthopaedic surgeon was Dr Botman ("Bone-man").

The next name needs some explanation.

I am a great opponent of fluoridation of the water supply. In these times of severe environmental pollution and overcharged immune systems, it is the epitome of folly to put a poison roughly as strong as arsenic in the water supply, in the (vain) hope that it will decrease tooth decay substantially.

Dr J. Colquhoun, a dentist from New Zealand and one of the world authorities on this subject, has demonstrated statistically that adult teeth in a fluoridated region are no better than those in an unfluoridated one.

As an opponent I am a subscriber to *Fluoride*, the highly scientific Journal of the International Society for Fluoride Research. It is full of articles about teeth, mouths, gums, in short, everything one sees when someone yawns.

In the November 1996 issue, the leading article was written by a man whose name was Bruce Spittle.

DATES

50% of my patients are children.

On 28 September 1995 two new little patients were scheduled, one directly after the other.

The first one was born on 15-5-1990. The complaint of the parents was "wild and uncontrollable behaviour".

The second one was born on 14-5-1990. The complaint of the parents was "wild and uncontrollable behaviour".

Not only did the complaints match but so did (nearly) the birthdays. A double coincidence, one could say.

"Duplizität der Fälle" the Germans call this phenomenon – "Doubling of Cases". It bedevils our consulting hours on a regular basis.

Here is another one.

New patients have to write a letter for an appointment, enclosing a description of their complaints. Usually we are encumbered by long waiting lists and then suddenly we have gaps and my assistant straight away rings the new patients and gives them appointments. That is why new ones normally come in small clusters.

So it happened that on 29-5-1997 she made two appointments for children, one at 2 p.m. and one at 2.30 p.m.

When she wrote the addresses on the patient cards she got slightly confused and thought she had made an error somewhere (an extremely rare occurrence).

Address of child A: Zeeuws Water 11 in Vijfhuizen.

Address of child B: Zeeuws Water 12 in Vijfhuizen.

(I have had to change the names for reasons of privacy, but it was the same street in the same municipality with only one difference in the house number.)

That afternoon when child A left my room, he and his mother ran into child B and her mother. The children knew each other, they played together, but the mothers had not known about the appointments with me, neither had they ever spoken to each other about me.

When my mother died we had to clear out the house where she had lived for 46 years.

On 29 September 1981 (please note the date) we had to tackle the attic where she kept all her old trunks. As she had regularly bought new ones and never thrown away the old ones, soon the back garden was littered with rather mouldy cases, boxes, bags, valises and trunks.

I opened them all, but did not find any hidden treasures. In one of them there was a daily paper which looked very old, so I took it home to show my wife.

When she looked at it, she pointed out that the date of this daily paper (the *Telegraaf*) was 29 September 1945, 3 months after the end of World War Two and liberation by the Allies.

A chance of one in 365, one could say, looking at it superficially, but that is not true. There was also the chance that no paper had been left in those trunks at all. Looking at it that way, the chance of such a thing happening was phenomenally small. No, it was a real coincidence and no mistake.

Sometimes I suspect coincidence of playing practical jokes.

In June 1989 we had rented an apartment near Salernes in Provence. The owner had restored the ruins of an old farmhouse and provided accommodation for four families.

On 28 June, my birthday, the chap next door on the left, an Englishman called Fred, said to me, "Tonight we'll have a birthday party."

I looked at the man a bit strangely. How, by Jove, had he

discovered my birthday and what a nice man he must be to organise the celebration.

My wife, always the practical one, afterwards said, "Of course it is *his* birthday."

Which proved to be the answer.

Fred was indeed a very pleasant man and, moreover, related to Tolkien's hobbits, as he gave away presents that evening to all and sundry, smilingly assisted by his charming wife, Cynthia. We had a great "double party".

A year later in June 1990 we returned to the same apartment.

Stimulated by Fred's good example (he was not there that year), I told another family next door, "Tonight we'll have a birthday party."

These people, Thorben and Renate, were very friendly Danes, but when I extended this invitation, a sort of troubled look came over Thorben's face. He looked at me a bit strangely and, after some hesitation, he carefully and circumspectly asked me if I had somehow happened to see his passport.

When I assured him that this was not the case, he relaxed and told me that today, 28 June, was his birthday and for a moment he had thought I was throwing a party for him.

Again we had a splendid feast with four families and the French owners of the house.

Two years in succession, two men and neighbours had shared the same birthday and the reaction of the two "victims" had been practically identical.

Before leaving the subject of dates one peculiar fact needs to be mentioned.

Important dates have a tendency to run in families. They occur in clusters. On one particular date one might find a birthday, a death, a marriage, etc.

On 3 July 1943 I stayed with my friend Gerrit in his country house outside Haarlem, near the dunes.

There was something odd about this house, built like an old manor house. When Allied planes bombed Cologne (142 miles away as the crow flies) during the night, the house silently shook on its foundations. Apparently, longitudinal vibrations through the earth ended there. It was an eerie experience.

In Dutch we have an expression for someone who is flabbergasted: "He looked as if he'd heard the thunder in Cologne." Well, I have heard it literally.

That beautiful summer evening, on 3 July, Gerrit said to me, "I will show you that girl I've told you about. She really is a dish. Come on, she lives next door."

We walked for ten minutes through their park and then across a beautiful garden towards a slightly smaller country house. There I met the girl and was not impressed. A bit later, her younger sister An walked into the room and we got on fantastically well.

This An was about to go to the school I had just graduated from. I told her a lot about it, imitated all the teachers and told her that she couldn't have made a better choice.

On 3 July 1948 she, too, graduated and she still has an impressive certificate with the date to prove that it really was that day.

This An subsequently became the mother of five children, four boys and a girl. The girl was born on 3 July 1959, exactly 11 years to the day after An's graduation and exactly 16 years after I met her mother for the first time. Elisabeth she is called and I couldn't have a better daughter.

Other people have noticed how dates cluster in their families and passed on their findings to me.

Numbers, dates, names and coincidences

NUMBERS

This last part of the chapter needs a somewhat more extensive explanation.

One of the men of genius whom I have had the honour to encounter in my life was a Hasidic Jew called Friedrich Weinreb. This man was in possession of a very old orally-transmitted tradition which taught Jews how to read the Old Testament. This knowledge had always been kept secret in certain Jewish families, which was not so difficult, as part of it was kept in living brains, and the part written down was in a slanting Hebrew script so small, that it could hardly be deciphered.

It was, however, Weinreb's view that we lived in such dangerous times that part of the secret teachings should be revealed to those who were interested in it, Jew or non-Jew, just to help them understand this bewildering age.

He justified this breach of secrecy with the following story:–

The scrolls kept under lock and key in the synagogue, which were only used for reading the Torah during services, were never meant to be seen by profane (non-Jewish) eyes. There was one exception. When there was a pestilence in town, the scrolls were openly carried around the city to ward off the evil.

That was why he was now prepared to reveal what had always been hidden. Those Jews who also knew the secrets were not altogether pleased.

For close on four years Weinreb was my teacher and one of the things he taught me to perfection was the significance of numbers.

I will give two examples to prepare the reader for the connection between a certain number and an amazing coincidence.

In Hebrew there is no difference between letters and numbers.

Aleph, the first letter of the alphabet, is also number 1 and when you see aleph standing alone, not incorporated in a word, you cannot say if an *A* or a 1 is meant. Beth is number 2 but the letters do not run from 1 to 22: the sequence is 1-2-3-4-5-6-7-8-9-10-20-30-40-50-60-70-80-90-100-200-300-400. Those are the numerical values of the 22 letters.

The numbers are not just curiosities but can tell you the significance of a word.

Let us start with something simple. The word for "father" in Hebrew is AB, 1-2 (= 3). It tells us that a man (1) marries a woman (now there are two) and that the sum total is the child (3).

The same idea is hidden in Pytharogas' famous formula:

$$A^2 + B^2 = C^2.$$

The square of the vertical side of a right-angled triangle added to the square of the horizontal side is equal to the square of the hypotenuse. Pythagoras goes deeper than the Hebrew word AB. In AB one simply sees the idea of a family implied in the word father: father-mother-child.

In Pythagoras the vertical side is the father, the horizontal side the mother, the hypotenuse the child. But they do not simply add up. The child is not just father + mother. In that case the equation would be $A + B = C$. Nor is the child just the product of its parents. In that case it would be $A \times B = C$.

No, all members, father and mother and child, fulfil themselves (are "squared") by giving the best they have. Each of them stays unique and free. Here is the principle of freedom.

But also, the three of them make a triangle. They are not three unattached sides, they form a community, a whole. And that is love. Freedom and love are two sides of the same coin.

Perhaps someone will ask, "What if there are more children?"

In these teachings each new child is considered as an only child – unique. Not no. 1, no. 2 or no. 3. One was not allowed to add up people as though they were apples in a basket or numbers on a payroll.

Here is the second example:–

In our Bible we find the expression "God Almighty". As Weinreb taught me, the word "Almighty" ("Shaddai" in Hebrew) is a contraction of three Hebrew words – : "He [that] says: Enough!"

The philosophy behind these words is this:

After Creation the world began to move away from God. It must be clear to observers that by now we have travelled quite a distance. It even looks as if an acceleration has taken place. Until about 200 years ago science still started with the maxim that the world had been created by an omniscient Creator. Physical laws could be discovered because an intelligent Creator had put them there in the first place.

The consensus in science has since then altered completely.

No Creator at the beginning any more, no Creation. Evolution is the all-encompassing paradigm of the 20th century. The Creator has been ousted from His Creation and forgotten.

We have reached a point as far away from God as possible.

There exists, according to the prophets of Israel, who foresaw this development long ago, a danger that the whole of Creation (under human leadership) will move so far away that it will be lost forever. So a safety valve has been built into the world which is hidden in the name Shaddai. At a certain moment when, spiritually speaking, things look hopeless, a Voice commands: "Enough!" The movement away from the origin alters course back towards it. In a diagram it is depicted as a circle:

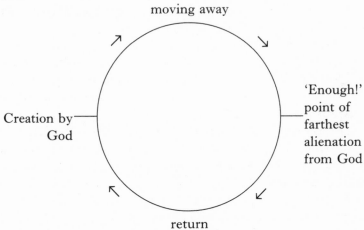

In numbers the name Shaddai is written: 300-4-10.

The numerical value of that word is 300 + 4 + 10 = 314.

Most people who have studied some mathematics at school will recognise it: 3, 14 (never mind the comma) is Pi, a symbol for the ratio of the circumference of a circle to the diameter; it makes a circular movement possible.

In this ancient science there still exists a unity between religion (God calling men back with the word "Enough!") and physical knowledge (the circle being defined by the symbol Pi).

Now for a number that has played a role in a remarkable coincidence – 58.

There is a name connected with this number: Noah, written N-Ch, 50-8. In Dutch we still have the same pronunciation of this name as in Hebrew, with the guttural "Ch" at the end.

Noah, the man who, with his family, was saved from the great Genesis Flood which covered the whole earth when the massive water "envelope" around our planet, high up in the stratosphere, broke.

Noah, the only one who found grace and was saved from the greatest calamity this planet has ever experienced, has a significant name. It is an anagram of Ch-N, "Chen", and this is the Hebrew word for "grace".

So in this name Noah there are hidden two significant ideas:

The absolute end of a period   (the Genesis Flood)
The saving grace of God   (Noah came through the flood
                                unscathed).

There exists a direct historical application of these principles. Written records of history suddenly appear around 6000 years ago all over the world. One could say that the civilisation now spread throughout much of the earth has its roots then.

We are now nearing the end of that civilisation. Not the end of mankind, or the world, but the end of the parameters that have been valid for the last 6000 years. We are on the brink of destroying many things that seemed destined to last and of embarking on something so new that we can hardly fathom it at present.

Elderly people can already understand something of that change as they have seen its beginning. During the last 60 years, our world has changed out of all recognition and for many of us it feels as if we are living on a new planet. But this is only the beginning, the real change is still to come.

Jewish circles, the same ones which kept so much of this knowledge hidden (probably for good reasons), know that this century is not like other centuries. How do they know this?

Christian chronology tells us that this is the 20th century, to be exact, the year of Our Lord 1997 as I write this.

Biblical chronology, which is also used by the Jews, has it that this is the year 5757. This is the *58th* century.

Many of the Biblical prophets talk about an "end time", some-

times called "the last days" (as in 2 Peter 3:3), and it might well
be that the 58th century is a good candidate for that apocalyptic event.

Having explained all this, let us return to our subject.

Remember the books I wrote for Mara?

The fourth book has as its principal person Jacqueline. I was rather
astonished to make her acquaintance, for she was not quite my type
when we first met. Jacqueline is a rather severe young woman, born
to Debora in the Alsace. She later emigrates to the Netherlands and
becomes a French teacher at a high school in Amsterdam.

Religiously speaking, she has a "one-tract" mind. Her favourite
argument is that if everyone kept the Ten Commandments, there
would be no trouble in this world.

One day during festivities at her school she meets a strange, small,
red-headed man who provokes her into uttering her usual pro-
nouncement about the Ten Commandments. He then says, "Let's
bet that you break them all before we are a couple of years further
down the road."

At first she refuses indignantly, but when he more or less accuses
her of cowardice, she rather scornfully agrees to the wager.

Then, suddenly, he vanishes.

Now follows a strange period in Jacqueline's life.

The story is set during World War Two.

Without being aware of it, she breaks the Ten Commandments one
after the other. How could she not know this?

Because the Commandments can be applied to a much wider field
than many people realise, as the Lord has already pointed out in the
Sermon on the Mount.

Stealing, for instance, is not only committing a burglary, but also
using someone's ideas without mentioning his name or publishing
someone's writings without his permission.

Killing is not just a physical act; the intention to kill is equally a
transgression. If something prevents the murder from actually taking
place, the Commandment has still been broken.

Every time Jacqueline breaks one of the Commandments she is
shortly afterwards transported to another time, thousands of years
ago in the past. She has completely forgotten that she is Jacqueline,
for there she is Princess Astra, daughter of a mighty ruler in the
Middle East.

Astra is quite the opposite of Jacqueline. Adventurous, rather wild,
unscrupulous, but also warm, true to her friends, original. She does
not mind breaking all the Commandments if it suits her and helps her
to get her own way.

Every time Astra clearly demonstrates which Commandment has been broken and when Jacqueline returns to her own time and her own awareness, she remembers her "Astra life" and suddenly realises that once again she has taken a step closer to losing her wager with the red-headed man.

As the story unfolds, two processes begin to run in parallel.

In Jacqueline's life it becomes clear that, for some reason unknown to herself, she is emotionally frozen and slowly but surely her story draws towards some terrible crisis.

Astra, her alter ego, apparently lives in the period just before the great Genesis Flood, which comes nearer and nearer. A gigantic personality overshadows her age, a strange man, ridiculed by all, who is building a large vessel on dry land and is called the "boat-prophet".

At the end in Astra's world the flood comes, drowning Astra, and, at about the same time, Jacqueline is flooded by a devastating memory. After that she changes into a woman who at last is whole, in a sort of chemical synthesis of herself and Astra.

The book about Jacqueline is a flood story, both literally and psychologically, and the spirit of Noah looms large in the background.

I wrote the book *Jacqueline* in 1995. In 1997 I was engaged in writing my memoirs, looking up things in my diary all the time. So I came across the day I had started to write *Jacqueline* and the day that I finished it. I had even made a note of the hours spent. More of less absentmindedly I calculated how much time I had needed for it and could hardly believe my eyes.

I had started on 7 June 1995 at 9 a.m. sitting in the garden in southern France.

I had finished the book at exactly 11 p.m. on 2 August 1995.

According to Biblical reckoning the new day begins at sunset (see Genesis 1: "And there was evening and there was morning, one day." Using this timescale I was about two hours into the 58th day of writing when I finished the book. The story suffused with the great Noah epic had taken 58 days – the numerical value of Noah himself – to develop.

The subject of the miracles in numbers is vast and I have hardly scratched the surface. Hopefully, though, I have given you an idea of how coincidences and numbers hang together.

Are all these dates, names, numbers just chaotically distributed and do we attach significance to something that is without meaning?

What in fact *is* chaos? Does such a thing as real chaos exist?

IN MAY 1997 I delivered a lecture on Genesis and told my audience that in the first sentence all three properties of creation were given: "In the beginning [= time] God created the heavens [= space] and the earth [= matter]." This was not my discovery, as I had read it in *The Genesis Record* by Henry M. Morris.

A friend of mind raised his hand and asked, "What about sound?"

This was an important question. Of course sound was there, present even before light, as when the narrative tells us: "And God *said* [my italics]: 'Let there be light.'" First the word sounded then light came.

In my possession there is a wonderful book which I bought in the sixties.

It is full of pictures photographed by the writer (Theodor Schwenk) himself and its title is *Sensibeles* (*Sensitive Chaos*).

He showed how the same basic forms were repeated again and again in nature. The whirl caused by a stick pushed into a fast-flowing brook looks remarkably like patterns in the bark of a tree, and some seashells are reminiscent of a vortex when we look at them underwater.

The most impressive pictures were those of sounds from an organ, a violin, a flute and a French horn, made visible by the changes taking place in a flame when struck by the vibrations. Exquisite forms emerge, echoing anatomical shapes like that of the spinal column, or the windpipe. It was as if one were witnessing the very act of Creation.

St John says that "all came into being through it [the Word] and apart from it not even one thing came into being which has come into being" (the literal "Concordant Version" translation).

Judging from Schwenk's pictures St John had not spoken a poetic or philosophic but a literal truth.

Schwenk was one of the pioneers of a new science that started slowly during the sixties and only gained momentum after 1977 (the year of the first conference on the subject). It became known as the chaos theory.

As there exists a close relationship between coincidence and chaos, I must elaborate a little here, though – to tell the truth – much of it is too difficult for me to understand, in particular, the mathematical part.

For information on this I will dip into a real gold-mine, the book *Chaos, Making a New Science* by James Gleick. I will also refer to 6 articles published in the German magazine *Raum & Zeit* (*Space & Time*) by Gabi Buhren.

9

4th Intermezzo

Chaos

The best way to explain those aspects of the theory relevant to our subject is to look at certain key-words in the new science.

THE BUTTERFLY EFFECT

"A butterfly stirring the air today in Peking can transform storm-systems next month in New York."

The idea behind this curious statement is this:–

According to the usual linear way of thinking an increasing force has an increasing effect. The harder I push the pedals of my bicycle, the faster I go.

But when one thinks in a non-linear way, one observes that a slight deviation at the start produces a huge effect at the finish. Though the simile is not exactly accurate, it is like a sledge-team walking with its dogs to the North Pole, a compass its only guide. The compass needs only to be a quarter of a degree out for them to miss the North Pole by a wide margin (if compasses work in those regions).

One of the maxims of this new science is that infinitesimal factors which have a tremendous impact are not unexpected nuisances. They do not happen once in a blue moon (making them, scientifically speaking, negligible), but they are the general rule, while neat and proper linear events are the exceptions. Or – to put it another way – disorder is the rule, order the exception.

Chaos theory of course has done no more than re-state a fact of life. From a seed no bigger than a peppercorn grows the largest tree on earth, the Californian Redwood or sequoia gigantica. From small, seemingly insignificant, events, whole cascades of other events can tumble forth, like a pebble high up in the mountains causing a devastating avalanche down in the valley.

What is the connection between the butterfly effect and our subject?

I mentioned it just now: not only in nature, but also in our daily lives, to all intents and purposes haphazard and minor events, can lead to an ever-growing series of other events. Not in a linear way, like dominos set closely together in a row, toppling over when the first one is given a slight push, but branching out like a tree, affecting many lives.

Gleick mentions in his book the well-known poem:

> "For want of a nail, the shoe was lost,
> for want of a shoe the horse was lost,
> for want of a horse the rider was lost,
> for want of a rider the battle was lost,
> for want of a battle, the kingdom was lost!"

The poem, however, arranges these events in a negative series. Often the chain of events is positive. Let me give an example.

As an introduction, let me first say something about water. 80% of our body is water, so pure water is a must for health, but water quality on the whole planet is deteriorating. For instance, 50 years ago, my home town of Haarlem still had about the best water in the Netherlands – rainwater filtered by the dunes – but since the industries in Amsterdam have used up too much of the water supply, water from the Rhine has been piped to the dunes and now we drink dune-water not completely purified of the extensive pollution found in the Rhine. Though the water company makes a gallant effort, it is not enough.

Important work on water has been done by an engineer in the employ of the French waterworks, Professor L. Cl. Vincent. This scientist had asked himself, "Apart from being free from bacteria, which parameters should be used to define good, drinkable water?"

He started by comparing the mortality rates in French districts with each other. There appeared to be considerable differences. He then tested the water in the different districts and discovered that water containing many *in*organic materials (i.e. straight from the soil itself, which is the sort of water we call "hard"), especially when it had been treated with chemical substances like chlorine, was found in the districts with the highest mortality rates. An example was the city of Paris.

On the other hand, water containing a minimum of organic salts (which he called "empty" water) coming from underground wells (e.g. the Massif Central) which had not been treated chemically, ran parallel with the lowest mortality rates (this was – to clarify the point – mortality from *all* illnesses).

Vincent kept secret the name of the small town where the average mortality rate per 100,000 inhabitants was *lowest* at 615 a year, while in Paris it was 1100 and in Roubaix 1520. Vincent feared that if the name of this town became known, there would be a massive move towards it.

Actually the town was Marset and people drink Volvic water, one of the cleanest mineral waters in existence (I have no shares in Volvic).

It flows out of their taps. So what exactly was good drinking water?

Vincent found three parameters:

The *acidity*. Water should be nearly neutral, tending slightly towards acidity with a pH of 6.8.

The *redox potential*. An electric value showing the amount of electrons.

The *electric resistance*, a measure of the amount of inorganic materials in the water (the more the worse).

By the way, human beings (and most animals) cannot metabolise inorganic materials. They are not food, only "grit" in the human and animal organism. Minerals should first be metabolised by soil bacteria.

Then they should be absorbed by the roots of plants, which metabolise the minerals further. Once they have become organic minerals, they are fit for consumption and can be eaten by animals and humans.

Water should be used to flush out sludge, not to bring dead minerals into the body.

When Vincent had finished his studies of water to his satisfaction, he made a jump that only men of genius make. He decided to test the three parameters he had established as indicators of good water on bodily fluids – blood, saliva and urine. He constructed a machine for measuring these parameters in a quick and efficient way and then began to test healthy volunteers in an attempt to map good health.

I came across this method early in 1985, was impressed by what I read and bought a machine from a Mr van Gestel, who imported them from Germany. When the machine has established the three parameters for blood, saliva and urine, the 9 numbers are then run through a computer. The results astonished me deeply.

From the elegantly drawn graph one could straightaway discern the health status of a patient. One could also assess in which direction this status deviated from the norm. Vincent called the thing you saw "le terrain", best translated as "the soil". One could see which "soil" the patient had (meaning the exact condition of his tissues). Was it acid or alkaline? Oxidized or reduced? Full of grit or clean?

When one saw the "soil", one could also evaluate what grew there best. Bacteria like an alkaline and reduced soil, moulds an acid and oxidized soil. Farmers usually know these things better than doctors. Even a town dweller like myself knows that daisies like a soil with a lot of calcium.

(By the way, the common daisy is a downright miracle, a tiny cyclotron converting calcium into potassium, as Louis Kervran from Paris has proved.)

Especially important in the graph was the alkaline and oxidized quarter, because here we find the three great illnesses of modern civilisation – cancer, thrombosis and viral infections.

The most difficult aspect of reading the graphs was to bear in mind that one measured health, soils, and possibilities, not specific illnesses. One had to learn to think in a completely new way.

On 2 October 1985 van Gestel brought me the machine and on 5 October, as if it had been planned, there was the first big conference in our region about the Vincent method in Keerbergen, Belgium.

When I parked my car in Keerbergen another car parked next to me.

It was Mr van Gestel's and I walked up to the house with him. I told him that, seeing how important pure water was to the Vincent method, I was glad that I had a reverse osmosis machine and pleased that it did not contain an organic filter, as that could develop into a bacteriological time-bomb. The machine had been sold to me by a Mr B.

"Mr B is at the conference to demonstrate his machine," he said. "Don't forget to ask him to show you the inside. It might be interesting." There was just the slightest edge to his voice. I looked at him but he had an absolutely deadpan face.

Mr B had assured me that the reverse osmosis machine contained only a mechanical filter. So, at the conference, during the coffee break, while there were a lot of people around, I asked him to show me the inside of the machine. He gave me a dirty look, but he could hardly refuse with everyone looking on and when he opened the bottom, next to the mechanical filter I detected a hidden organic filter.

I ordered him to come to my house as soon as possible and when he came, I told him to take out the organic filter, which had been there for two years. Under the microscope I found extensive yeast contamination. It would have been only a matter of time before intestinal trouble would have plagued us. I threw B out and bought a new machine whose (necessary) secondary filter could easily be replaced every three months.

But I also thought about van Gestel.

I had learned a lot about that man in the short time that I had walked with him from the car park to the house where the conference was being held.

In the first place he was knowledgeable.

In the second place he was honest, giving me that slight hint that my enthusiasm was misplaced.

In the third place he was discreet and did not want to accuse B outright of deception.

This very brief exchange of words showed me that the man was trustworthy. This led to a whole cascade of consequences.

With the appearance of the Vincent machine in my practice, it was, to use the words of my French colleagues, "as if intuition had obtained eyes". Thousands of patients could be helped with the new method but I had to adapt my whole therapeutic arsenal and many of the necessary remedies were not officially registered in my country and had to be imported from foreign countries.

My poor assistant, already pushed to the limit of her endurance in a busy practice, now had the additional burden of all sorts of bureaucratic regulations, which involved a lot of paperwork and occasionally a bit of smuggling. She began to look haggard.

It was then that I remembered the reliability of Mr van Gestel. I suggested to him that he organise the whole import of non-registered remedies, smuggling not included, and from that time on he became absolutely indispensable to my practice and not only to mine. Many of my colleagues and even a lot of pharmacists began to make use of him.

So, coming back to the poem, it seemed that a chance meeting in a car park and a chance remark from me about the water-filter first saved my health, and then later on led to intensive cooperation involving many medical doctors, close on a hundred pharmacists, thousands of patients and the lifting of an impossible burden from my assistant's shoulders.

One "seed moment" had become a tree with many branches.

So here we see the positive version of the horse-shoe ditty:

Thanks to a chance remark a machine was opened.

Thanks to an opened machine a man was proved trustworthy.

Thanks to a man proven trustworthy a remedy for chaos was found.

Thanks to remedies officially becoming available thousands of sick people were helped.

Thanks to thousands of sick people being helped thousands of families lived happier lives.

One asks oneself where such a cascade ends.

Is this just luck?

When Napoleon had to appoint a new general he used to ask the applicant, "What sort of military career have you had?"

The man, of course, would extol his military education and experience.

Then Napoleon would ask, "Have you been lucky with your battles?"

If the general said, "A couple of times I have – through no fault of my own – been plain unlucky", Napoleon's response would be, "I cannot give you the job, because luck is a quality of a man's character."

There is indeed something special about luck: one has to grasp it when it is offered. This is what Shakespeare says in *Julius Caesar* (iv:3):

> "There is a tide in the affairs of men,
> which taken at the flood leads on to fortune."

So what is new in the butterfly effect? Haven't we always known it?

Yes, but in the affairs of men, not in physical sciences. The butterfly effect as part of the weather forecast is a new development.

What is new is that, in this time of computers and super-exact measurements, we have found this "sign of life" in so-called inanimate nature. It is as if the time of the fairies is coming back; as if the soul is returning to nature after its long Descartian absence.

In the 20th century the butterfly has been immortalised as the symbol of the soul by Elisabeth Kübler Ross. She has used this symbol ever since she travelled through Germany directly after the Second World War and visited the concentration camp Sobibor. There she saw on the walls many butterflies, drawn or carved by children the evening before they were gassed.

The butterfly effect only *seems* haphazard; in reality it is a mysterious law of life at work. In human affairs it creates new events and possibilities. In nature it aids adaptation and maintenance, not new creation, because really new things do not appear in our world. Creation stopped after humanity was made.

The human being, however, is meant to continue evolving, and that is why new things do happen in our lives. Not in the lives of caterpillars, woodpeckers or gorillas. They are finished produces while we are still being moulded and shaped, whether we like it or not.

FRACTALS

If the world is not linear, contrary to the long-held beliefs of materialistic scientists, what is it?

Mandelbrot, the trail-blazer of chaos theory coined this new word, which in essence means "broken". Original surfaces are not smooth but rough, coastlines are not flowing but full of bays and capes.

When reading about the pioneers of chaos theory I discovered that the most important scientists in this field were Jews. Apart from Mandelbrot there is that other intellectual giant, Feigenbaum. I mention just two, there are several others.

Now why would the idea of a world being fractal, broken into little pieces, originate in Jewish minds? Or: "What is the strange (or hidden) attractor" to use their words (see next part).

99

For 3500 years the Torah has been the centre of their ancestors' lives. How does the Torah begin? With the word "In the beginning". I say word, because in Hebrew it is *one* word – Bereshith.

The Hebrew Bible hardly knows capital letters but one of the glaring exceptions is the first letter of the Bible. The original text begins with a capital B (the Hebrew letter "Beth"). As I explained before, this is also the number 2. This means that at Creation an original unity was broken. Creation from God's point of view is breaking and that is why the idea of sacrifice is inherent in the beginning of this world (" . . . the lamb slain from the foundation of the world" Rev. 13:8).

Thus it was not a poetic streak in these Jewish pioneers that made them the first to find creation hidden in brokenness. They simply expressed their old faith in a new way.

Do not misunderstand me. I am not saying that they projected the old faith onto the modern world, adjusting the "broken-world" model to fit the 20th century. Far from it. On the contrary, they were the selected few who were able to recognise the brokenness in our universe, while other scientists still clung to the old mechanical world view, and they could do this because it was an aspect of their spiritual inheritance.

This being split into two, the initial 2 of the Torah, is a fact of life. It has also been found by another chaos scientist, May. Working with non-linear models he discovered that one of their main characteristics is bifurcation. His tool was a normal calculator and he worked with abstract numbers. Of course every biologist knows this basic fact of life: from a single fertilized cell come first 2, then 4, then 8, then 16, etc. new cells, until trillions of cells form the human body through a process of endless bifurcation. The chaos-theorists have not so much found a new principle as re-phrased an ancient one.

It will be clear to the reader that there exists a direct relevance to our subject. In chaos theory two (or more) independent series of numbers meet and form beautiful pictures on the computer screen as we shall see in section 3 below. In coincidence two or more independent events "fall together", forming a surprising whole.

When I say that two independent factors meet I have left something out. Both in chaos theory and in real-life coincidences, seemingly unconnected factors form something new and beautiful, but what puts them together?

In real life we do not know: in the case of the computer one would say the man who puts the numbers in. However, it has been discovered that there is a third, hidden, force involved. It weaves the series of numbers into a miraculous "living" forms. This hidden force is the third maxim of chaos theory the "hidden attractor".

THE HIDDEN ATTRACTOR

For someone born in 1925 computer language is still highly esoteric, while my grandchildren play with computers as if they were pet animals. Without the computer the strange attractors never would have been found. What I have understood with my scant insight is the following:–

Certain data are fed as numbers to a computer. They are derived from, for instance, some dynamic system like water beginning to boil (expansion, temperature, etc.).

Then one lets these numbers play with each other. They are multiplied with each other and the result, the output, is used as input. A sort of inbreeding. The results are not projected on the screen as series of numbers but as pictures, images, or graphs.

To the great surprise of observers, what has been found is that, instead of rubbish heaps or intangible senseless threads or clods, after enough repeats dream-like pictures evolve and it becomes clear that somewhere there is a hidden organiser, who bends and twists these images into their beautiful forms like an invisible potter at work.

We know that these things happen in real life all the time. In cell-multiplication we observe this hidden organising principle, which makes from the original cell not one great lump but a beautiful natural form like a rose, a peacock or a blooming baby.

Sometimes in pregnancy something seems to go wrong with the organiser and instead of a baby we actually see a big lump of cells without shape, called a mola.

In the computer models this hidden organiser sometimes reveals a brief glimpse of himself, like Hitchcock showing himself fleetingly in one of his thrillers.

Before the eyes of the fascinated observers a breathtaking panorama unfolds on the screen. The most famous one is Mandelbrot's composite figure called the Mandelbrot set, or "Apple-man". It emerged when he took a number, multiplied it by itself, added the original number, fed the sum total back into the computer and repeated the process thousands of times. After at least 10,000 times (all the while carefully pruning those branches that tended to vanish into eternity, keeping the picture within visible boundaries), this composite picture emerged as a round image, sprouting images of itself on a smaller scale at its margins, and these small replicas themselves also sprouted similar images on a still smaller scale.

But this was not all. At the margins stunningly beautiful structures emerged like the most sophisticated underwater pictures of a coral reef and its inhabitants. One of the structures was even called the sea-horse and there was also the immensely detailed eye of the seahorse.

Sometimes a tiny black blob appeared within these dream-like animals and then, when the computer blew it up to make it more visible (as apparently can be done), a new complete Appleman appeared.

It was as if Mandelbrot had looked into the hidden kitchen of the Creator and on a two-dimensional scale had tuned into the creating process described in Genesis 1.

This was one side of the coin. The other side was even more astonishing. The images were all self-referential on a different scale but none was identical. Mandelbrot had hit upon one of the great mysteries of life – its endless variability. Identical things do not exist in creation, save perhaps in the sick minds of scientists who want to clone animals or even men, or in the hands of totalitarians who love nothing more in their subjects than uniformity. In nature, however, uniformity is a non-entity. No two leaves on a tree are the same. No identical twin is really identical.

I observed this same fact in my study of angels. Many experiences bore similarities, like the vision of two angels near a protected person, but identical stories did not exist. The very variability proved to me that I was confronted with real experiences.

The computer images only develop when at least three independent factors work on each other. For creation three forces have to co-operate.

Nearly all religions know this number 3 as being connected with the creative process. Moreover in the emerging pictures the whole is always present in every part. This is also the case in a hologram and, according to the latest discoveries, in that most mysterious and intricate instrument to be found on earth, the human brain.

In acupuncture one can see something similar. The whole of the human body is represented in the shell-like structure of the ear, just like a small Appleman growing on the large one. Perhaps the Appleman is a universal symbol, like the composite symbol of the ten sephiroth. A consequence of chaos science is that we can now demonstrate the truth of ancient sayings using technical methods which to modern minds is always more convincing than simple faith.

I do not mean this to sound cynical. It has apparently become necessary to follow this mechanical path. Today's generation has to be yelled at loudly and clearly when it comes to spiritual truths.

Let us always be aware, though, that the computer only shows shadows of the truth. They are *not* the truth, because in every case too much has been left out, beautiful as the pictures are. It is not the real world we are seeing but something more like the holodeck of the Starship Enterprise.

What we observe at the margins of the Appleman looks like teeming life (without real life vitalising it) and again we see the relevance to our subject.

If virtual reality seems to indicate a teeming life at the margins, reality itself registers an enhancement of life when coincidence strikes. During a really good coincidence, which happens at the margins of our seemingly logical existence, the quality of life is improved.

There is a feeling of uplift, a buoyancy. That is the reason why people like to talk about them. "Listen to what happened to me today!" Cheeks glow, eyes sparkle.

Some researchers went one step further than Mandelbrot, who let a single formula replicate itself. They played a heads-or-tails random game to determine which numbers were going to be fed to the computer.

Again, instead of utter chaos, splendid life-like structures emerged. At once one is reminded of the heads-or-tails method in the *I Ching* which seems a random business and yet has helped people to see structure in a life that threatened to become formless.

SCALE

One of the conclusions Mandelbrot drew from his findings was that the world has scale. His big Appleman sprouted little Applemen who sprouted tiny Applemen ad infinitum. Using his computer is pictorialised an old idea about the world which has been extensively described by Maurice Nicoll in his *Commentaries on the Teachings of Gurdieff and Ouspensky*.

In this ancient model the whole of creation is seen as a musical octave. Creation itself in this system is not instantaneous (no more than in Genesis) but takes place on a descending scale, each note symbolising a lower dimension on the scale.

When we talk about the octave we usually say, "Do-re-mi-fa-sol-la-si-do." We inhabit a world that is finished and look up (at least that is what we hope).

Creation is symbolised by the descending octave: do-si-la-so-fa-mi-re-do. Nicoll places a dimension next to every note:

DO = the creative will of God
SI   = the sidereal world, all galaxies together
LA = our particular galaxy – a branch perhaps
SOL = our particular sun in our galaxy – a side branch
FA = the family of planets, surrounding our sun
MI = the earth as a twig from the planetary branch
RE = our moon, one scale lower than the earth

(Perhaps that is the reason why the travellers to the moon look like deep-sea divers).

Nicoll says that spiritual development is impossible without an understanding of scale. Mandelbrot has done a great service to mankind in bringing back to science the awareness of scale.

It is understandable that a consciousness of scale is related to spiritual development. Since the French Revolution there has been a great emphasis on equality. Of course, the ideal of equal chances is an admirable one, but the slogan has increasingly deteriorated into:

"You're no better than I am."

"Who do you think you are anyhow?"

"Who is God to tell me what to do? I didn't ask to be here."

During the French Revolution the desire that everyone should be absolutely equal (generalized in the 20th century) was implemented in a literal way: each head which was a little bit too high was chopped off.

The idea of political equality is beneficial and has been partly realised in our Western democracies, but the dark side is that we have lost our sense of scale and with it our feeling of awe. When nothing is higher than me I cannot be uplifted and this is, or should be, our aim. All religious systems agree on this point.

Though we can learn a lot from the octave as explained by Nicoll, in my view, there exists a fundamental flaw in the symbol.

It suggests that every note in the scale is of a greater or lesser dimension. The note Fa (all planets together) is a higher realm than the note Mi (our earth), and the note Sol (our sun) is one dimension higher than that of the planets. Moreover there is the suggestion that these are steps on a spiritual scale. This of course makes no sense. It would mean that mere bigness, mere adding of more matter, results in higher spirituality. The only real jump from spirit to matter can be found in the highest Do (God's creative will) to Si (the galaxies taken together).

In the Hebrew system this mistake is not made. There, everything that can be observed with the senses (in our time, with the help of our sophisticated instruments) is still "earth", the lowest realm. I have not thought this out all by myself. It was C. S. Lewis who first pointed out to me in one of his books that we must not be daunted by mere vastness or distance. "We shall outlive the galaxies," he says somewhere. So as a symbol of scales the octave is an elegant one, but it should be seen as a parable, not as stark reality. On the other hand, the idea of creation being related to a musical scale is magnificent and I believe quite true.

Mandelbrot calls scale the signature of life. In other words, by considering his Appleman with every more Applemen on an ever-diminishing scale we can restore in ourselves our lost sense of scale. Then our soul becomes part of a larger soul (the original Adam, or "Adam Kadmon", as he is called in Hebrew lore) and this archetypal Adam, or humanity as it is spread out in time and space, is said to be made originally "in the image of God" (though at the beginning something went wrong) and with that "image of God" we sense a still higher scale, a being embedded in an incomprehensible whole.

These are humbling thoughts and humbleness in ancient and less barbaric civilisations than ours was considered a positive quality.

What has scale to do with coincidence?

Everything. It might even be part of the explanation.

I return to the versatile ideas of Ouspensky. In his Book *A New Model of the Universe* he describes a group of political prisoners incarcerated in a grim prison on an island in the midst of Lake Ladoga (near St Petersburg in Russia).

They are in solitary confinement and maintain contact with each other by knocking on the water-pipes. They have long philosophical talks and one day one of them discourses on the fourth dimension. He reminds his friends of the fact that outside the prison there exists a wide expanse of water and he continues, "Imagine that on the surface of this lake there lives a two-dimensional rational entity. One day someone goes for a swim. First he walks into the water and our two-dimensional being suddenly sees how, out of nowhere, two circles appear in his world. They are of course the places where the surface water surrounds the legs of the man who is going for a swim. [Doesn't it remind us of the mysterious crop-circles that appear out of nowhere?] When the man wades deeper into the water up to his middle, the two-dimensional being observes how the two circles mysteriously become one. At last with a splash the man dives under water and the two-dimensional being sees first how the big circle changes into a complicated form and then vanishes altogether. In a short time he has experienced three miracles."

The speaker then proceeds to draw a comparison between our three-dimensional world and the 4th dimension. Just as in a world of two dimensions an intrusion from the 3rd dimension is seen as a miracle, so to us three-dimensional beings an intrusion from the 4th dimension must seem miraculous.

It could well be that those small miracles we call coincidences are in reality glimpses of a larger, four-dimensional world. They are felt to be real but they are too large for us to understand. In any case they enhance our sense or scale and that is good for our souls.

DEFINITIONS OF CHAOS

We will end this journey through the chaos theory with quotations from the writings of some researchers into chaos.

"Chaos is structured."

This sounds like "black is white" but it is an empirical reality. These scientists have simply observed it.

"Chaos is creation of information."

What is meant here is that chaos bridges the gaps between the differences in scale. These gaps are of great importance.

In the great composite symbol of the sephiroth we see 22 "paths" bridging the gaps between the ten principles. These paths are symbolised both by one of the 22 letters of the Hebrew alphabet and by the 22 trumps in the Tarot. All these symbols are there to help in bridging the gaps.

In Nicoll's great octave the gaps between the notes are the normal intervals known in music. Nicoll stresses the fact that the half-intervals between Fa and Sol and between Mi and Do are of paramount importance.

In the development of a human being, which (hopefully) is an upward process, these half-intervals represent difficulties to be overcome, hindrances to be struggled with.

Every car driver can understand how a narrowing on a busy road produces a traffic jam. The half-intervals are seen as a narrowing on the road of life. They give a lot of trouble but, having struggled through them we find we have learnt more in a month than in a smooth two-year period.

Not only in a single human life do we see how this law of the half-intervals actively operates. Time and again I have seen how a group or an association, working towards a common goal, after an initial flying start, slowly but surely gets entangled in such a half-interval.

Recognising this moment and using it as a challenge can save the day and even bring the group or association onto a higher and better level. On the other hand, ignoring it eventually leads to disaster.

This is what can be read into the strange statement that "chaos is creation of information". At the moment when chaos is recognised, one must not despair but try to extract the information hidden in the situation.

"*Chaos is health.*"

To my mind this also means that linear uniformity breeds disease. Let me explain this apodictic statement:

By now it must be clear that what we call chaos is a bubbling source of ever-new possibilities and experiences. It is from here that artists draw their inspiration; it is their connection with this source that makes young children so adorable, fresh, and sometimes exasperating.

Our culture is one that stresses the importance of freedom, especially in education. This over-emphasis should make us suspicious, for under the cloak of freedom often lurks the fanatical totalitarian ruler.

Here are three quotations from John Taylor Gatto who in 1990 was named New York City's Teacher of the Year.

"Children and old people are penned up and locked away from the business of life."

"It is absurd and anti-life to be part of a system that compels you to sit in confinement with people of exactly the same age and social class. That system effectively cuts you off from the immense diversity of life and the synergy of variety. It cuts you off from your own past and future, sealing you in a continuous present, much the same way television does."

"The truth is that schools don't really teach anything except how to obey orders."

(A speech by John Taylor Gatto, *Hope Magazine*, Vol. 1, no. 4, Sept./Oct. 1996.)

There it all is: the uniformity of linear thinking, the lack of chaos, the will to exercise power.

The consequences are grave. Life tastes stale for many youngsters and the suicide rate amongst them is a matter for concern.

Of course I realise that Gatto speaks for the USA and that things are not too bad in many schools, but he is a whistle-blower, warning of a general trend, and we'd do well to listen to his words.

One of the methods of reducing men to grey uniformity is to identify them by number only. One of the first things that happened in a concentration camp was the tattooing of a number on the skin. It was dehumanisation pure and simple. This is a sin against the Holy Ghost, denying that the other person is a human being, made in the image of God. A dictator does not want to know that every human being is unique. There is only one unique person in a dictatorship and that is the dictator himself.

This is my apologia for the categorical statement that uniformity makes us sick. It does not belong to creation and it does not belong to us. And that is why a chaos scientist said, "Chaos is health". To allow as much originality as possible in every one of us is healing for our gravely sick civilisation.

"*Chaos (disorder) is channelled into patterns with some underlying theme.*"

Splendid, but who is doing the channelling? What is the hidden attractor?

"*Odd shapes carry meaning.*"

A generation that believed in tidy mathematical shapes built our hideous 20th-century towns. They degrade the human being who pants for irregularity and pleasant surprises. Every man knows that a perfectly symmetrical woman is boring to distraction.

"*Hidden forms fill the universe.*"

Here we are reminded of Jesod, the foundation, the aethereal world and also the world of ideas postulated by Plato.

"*Non-linearity (structured chaos) is a defence against noise.*"

The term "noise" is a technical one, coming from electro-magnetic science. In the thirties, when radios began to appear in our homes, now and then a yelping noise was transmitted. For some reason or other it was called "the Mexican Dog".

The above statement suggests that chaos absorbs "noise".

Applying the statement to daily life, nowadays we know that noise is a great health hazard. In those living near airports more high blood pressure has been reported. The TV of the neighbours at 1 a.m. can drive people almost to murder. How could chaos or non-linearity help in those cases? Are there in fact creative solutions to these problems and other instances of hindrance?

It is amazing how versatile people can be when they realise that a normal solution is impossible and they use their imagination.

I remember how one of my children, a light sleeper, always woke up late at night because a rather deaf old man in the house next door had turned up the TV to full volume. His room was next to her bedroom and a nice request did not help. I had at that time a little electric machine for curing warts. It shot out sparks like beautiful little blue electric tongues.

When, once, my daughter could not sleep I held the machine near an iron bedpost and began to make the nice blue tongues. Immediately there was a great commotion in our neighbour's room. Apparently what I hoped had indeed happened: the picture on the screen had disintegrated.

I had to repeat the procedure another night and then he got the message. The psychological effect on my daughter moreover was miraculous. Instead of crying pitifully that again she could not sleep, she had great fun and experienced a sort of liberation.

I see noise disturbance as an intolerable infringement on another man's freedom. Non-linear illogical processes are related to freedom.

It is freedom that pervades the whole of creation, from the erratic movements of molecules (Brownian movement) to the creative thoughts of a philosopher.

Why is freedom such a corner-stone in our Creation? Because without freedom love is impossible and love is the real purpose of creation.

Perhaps by now there are readers who think that I am all for chaos and anarchy. Nothing can be farther from the truth. What I believe is that there must be a framework of discipline and that within this framework there must be a lot of space for creative energy. Every tree must keep to its own form, a beach must remain a beach, an oak an oak. There is the *discipline*. On the other hand, each individual tree has the freedom to grow in its own particular way. There is the *freedom*, the mainspring of Creation's endless variety.

Real anarchy is trying to force the barriers open and, for instance, mix genes from one species with another. Genetic manipulation is the ultimate anarchy.

"Chaos is the reconciliation of free will with determination."

No need to expand on this one, I have just said as much.

All these statements sound less like the dry utterances of scientists, than religious confessions. Are science and religion approaching each other again after having gone their separate ways for centuries? Their meeting would indeed be a colossal coincidence.

It is, by the way, not my exclusive idea that chaos theory and coincidence have much in common.

Gleick talks about d'Arcy Thomson who discovered that ink droplets, falling into clear water, disperse themselves in such a way that a picture emerges looking remarkably like a living jellyfish.

He asks himself if this is just a casual coincidence, but on the next page he talks about purpose and though he leaves the conclusion to the reader the words are there.

Could coincidence be the name given to a hidden purpose? If so, whose purpose? And how many times did we miss the boat on account of not recognising the purpose?

If this is true, we are like sailors waiting for the right tide. That is why thinking about coincidence is so important, because in doing so we make ourselves more alert and we miss fewer fortunate chances.

Perhaps someone will ask why I do not talk about unfortunate coincidences. I do not deny that they exist but I am convinced that on the whole the phenomenon of coincidence is benevolent. Chaos theory shows beautiful forms underlying this reality, not hideous ones. Love and beauty are the building-blocks of creation.

And so the wheel of science has turned full circle.

Genesis 1 says that God at the beginning created the heavens and the earth.

What is described here is the creation of a fully structured cosmos.

The second sentence, however, says that the earth was without form and void and darkness was upon the face of the deep.

These words "without form and void" are in Hebrew "tohuvabohu" and have been translated in many different ways. "Irrsal and wirrsal," says Martin Buber, "chaos and mess". As a matter of fact, these words are themselves a mess. No one knows exactly what tohuvabohu means. Everything is upside down.

Wise men have reasoned that this does not equate with the facts mentioned in the first sentence. Apparently, while order still ruled in the heavens, something had gone wrong with the earth. They postulate that this was the time of the great rebellion by angels mentioned in the Book of Revelation. This is the so-called "gap theory", adhered to by some, refuted by others.

Finally (if there is truth in the gap theory) God *re*created the earth in the six "days" of Genesis. I put days in quotation marks as the word "Jom", day, can also mean a period.

What we have found is this:

Original cosmos → Chaos → New Cosmos.

The interesting thing is that science has gone the opposite way.

In the positive and optimistic days of Isaac Newton, Creation was seen as a world running like a clock. It had been wound up by the Creator during the six days' Creation and now it ran all by itself. "God's in His Heaven and all's right with the world," could only have been said in an optimistic age.

Then along came Freud, destroying our psychological certainty,

Darwin seemingly destroying our ancestry, Curie destroying the immunity of the earth's elements and Einstein finally destroying the solidity of time itself and with it Newton's smoothly-running world-clock.

From the new cosmos, going backward, we had entered tohuvabohu and the whole of human history began to reflect our bewilderment.

And now, while we begin to destroy the earth with great abandon on a scale larger than has ever been witnessed in human memory, scientists begin to discover a new structure behind chaos, more beautiful than we could ever have imagined. The first glimpses of the world even farther backwards, behind the second sentence of Genesis, begin to emerge.

This is the world made in the beginning, or, as another translation of the word "Beresthit" makes possible, "In His head."

"In His head God created heaven and earth". That is why some serious thinkers say that what our sensory organs show us is not a solid world, but a hologram in God's mind, each point reflecting the whole (see Michael Talbot's book *The Holographic Universe*).

Science, taking an opposite direction from creation, works ever more backwards and has now finally arrived at a point where it can glimpse the beginning:

New cosmos → Chaos → Original cosmos.

Chaos in itself is not creative, it is a creative stage. For the bewildered scientists at the end of the 19th and the beginning of the 20th century, when everything solid seemed to evanesce, chaos was also a state of mind. In that state absurdities like the "Big Bang" and "primeval slime" could be postulated. Now chaos scientists begin to draw back the veil over the scientific mind and the original structure becomes visible.

Perhaps a way can be found to reconcile those who believe in the gap theory − the fall of the angels between the first and second sentences of Genesis 1 − and those who refute such an idea.

To my mind, there is no need to let the angels fall at this point. Nor to postulate a sort of cosmic war, which devastated the earth and made it tohuvabohu. There is a much more elegant scheme that can put all minds at rest.

Look at the caterpillar. At a certain moment it stops eating and pupates. Within the pupa the original caterpillar body deliquesces. If one opens the pupa one finds unstructured slime, chaos. Yet from that deliquescent body is made an entirely new butterfly.

Could it be that a similar thing happened in creation? We would then have the following sentence:–

I. Genesis 1, first sequence

"In the beginning God created the heavens and the earth."

Or, at a deeper level of translation: "In His head God created the heavens and the earth." It ties in with the first sentence in John: "In the beginning was the word."

This is the original blueprint. The first cosmos.

II. "The earth was [sometimes translated as 'became'] without form and void" (tohuvabohu).

The original blueprint now has to be given form and substance. This second stage was a sort of pupation. It did not happen in the heavens but on earth and by that is meant that it happened to everything material. There was a big melt-down.

During that stage the same sentence in Genesis says that the spirit of God "hovered" over the face of the waters. This word "hovers" is a strange word, because in Hebrew it is derived from the word for spirit. "Spirited" would be a more precise translation, but it has an association in our minds with "spirited away" and so cannot be used. In any case this "hovering" is not a passive floating, but an active engagement. That is why some Hebrew commentators say "like a dove over its nest."

Could "hovered" perhaps be translated as "hatched"?

In other words, it might well be that during this second stage of Creation the Creator brought part of the original cosmos into a state of metamorphosis. The tohuvabohu stage then, would be the first part of that process, deliquescence of the original structure.

III. Now let us follow the building stages of the metamorphosis (the word means "going beyond the original form", as caterpillars turn into butterflies). These stages, totalling six, are described in the rest of Genesis 1.

This scheme shows clearly that it is not chaos itself that is the creative factor. It is a stage in the creative process.

When we believe in God the Creator, there is no problem. When we refuse to believe in Him, we are in trouble. Chaos becomes a force in itself. We have confused the effect with its Maker. It is then that we begin to believe in a Big Bang as the beginning of everything.

That is what happened to the scientific mind. The chaos at the turn of the century was a veil over the mind.

Science travelling backwards entered this tohuvabohu around the middle of the last century and the confusion became so intense that Nietzsche pronounced the death of God.

Wells calls this time "The Great Age of Confusion" (see his book *Men like Gods*).

But if we do not let ourselves be side-tracked by false conclusions drawn from the 19th-century tohuvabohu, we can recognise the apparent chaos of Genesis 1 (second sentence) as a hatching phase, an active process between two creative stages. There is perhaps primeval slime, but we can also discern the "Hatching Bird" (the Holy Spirit).

Science at last seems to have reached the end of the tunnel. The Big Bang will soon become the Big Surprise.

Chaos

So chaos theory has brought us a bit nearer to answering the question: "WHAT IS COINCIDENCE?"

It is another, higher, world or dimension breaking through into our world.

Two seemingly unconnected events in our world already form a unity in that higher world. We could not grasp it only because our minds are too limited.

Before we reach a final conclusion, though, we have to examine some more aspects of our subject. Only with a lot of information may the answer crystallize in our minds.

AT HIGH SCHOOL I was friendly with a boy called Jan van Manten (not his real surname). This was in 1942. He was rather taken by a girl called Elisabeth but then he fell in love with a certain Hetty Pom (not her real name). Another of our classmates called Bob, later a radiologist in Haarlem, made up a little song about the situation using a tune popular at the time:

> "O Jan van Manten,
> Why do a thing like that?
> You fell in love with Hetty Pom,
> Forgot Elisabeth."

In January 1994 my assistant said to me, "I've had a letter from a woman in Brussels. She wants to visit you for some medical advice."

I answered, "Send her to Ton."

This Ton is a friend of mine living near Brussels and he is a remarkably good physician. So my assistant sent her to Ton.

Have you ever had the experience of waking up in the morning with a little tune jingling in your head? This happened to me on 26 January 1994 and it was the Jan van Manten song of 52 years ago, complete with words. Whatever I did that day, it kept nagging me and either I found myself whistling or humming the tune or it sounded in my head, buzzing around like a wasp imprisoned in a room.

Then, in the late afternoon, my friend Ton rang me from Belgium.

"I have seen that woman, Mrs A, whom you referred to me. Did you know that she is the daughter of an old schoolfriend of yours?"

"Whoever do you mean?" I asked. "I don't know the name."

"No, she is married, but her maiden name is van Manten and her father's name is Jan."

The song left me straightaway, having performed its task.

Apparently time does not exist for the strange events we call coincidence.

On 10 November 1988 I visited my neighbour after dinner for his birthday celebration. There was a room full of people and at a certain moment the conversation became general and the subject was the Yeti in the Himalayas, also known as the abominable snowman, and his hairy cousins in California, Big Foot, those legendary, bigger-than-human, ape-like and yet intelligent beings.

What were they? Did they really exist? Were they just folk tales? A hoax perhaps? Or, if they did exist, why had no one ever caught one? In our century with all its modern technology it seemed hardly possible that such striking beings remained undiscovered still.

Not to mention our own dear "Nessie" (the Loch Ness monster) of course.

Returning home that evening, I pressed a button on my TV at random and there, on Discovery Channel, just starting at that moment, was a documentary about Yeti and Big Foot. Huge footprints in the snow were shown where the Yet had roamed in the Himalayas and eye witnesses in California were interviewed, who said they had met Bit Foot at close quarters.

The elusive beings had silently crept into the web of coincidence.

On 30 August 1984 a woman visited my office accompanied by her 1½-year-old daughter. The child played on the floor while the mother described her own complaints. When the medical part of her visit was finished, we just talked for a couple of minutes, as she had been my patient ever since she was a small girl herself. She mentioned her school and told me how exasperated she had been with geometry, for instance, with that dratted Pythagoras theorem.

I told her that there was a very practical way to explain that theorem, which I had just learned from a schoolchild:–

Square a + square b = square c.

Take a right-angled triangle. Make every side into the base of a square. Plant potatoes in the three squares. The produce from the square erected on the hypotenuse will equal that of the produce of the two other squares taken together: $A^2 + B^2 = C^2$.

She began to laugh and said that for the first time she had understood the theorem and she wondered why they had not told her this at school.

In my room I have a little box containing small cards in alphabetical order with interesting non-medical facts. The little toddler had managed to get hold of this and had taken out a card, which she proudly brought to her mother, while she was still laughing at my simple explanation. The mother gave a cry, snatched the card from the child, and said, "I'm awfully sorry."

She went over to the box to put back the card and stared with astonishment at the word on the first card confronting her – Pythagoras.

The old philosopher would have liked the story.

In order to understand the next incident the reader will have to absorb a slightly longer story.

In 1970 I received a visit from a Doctor E. He was a psychiatrist in the medical department of Haarlem's Health Service.

I knew him quite well as we were both on the board of a foundation concerned with education.

He told me that he and some other people were going to start a – for our country – unique project.

A certain Joshua Bierer had in the UK discovered that long-term psychiatric patients who spend years in psychiatric hospitals sometimes end up suffering not so much from their original illness as from the effects of their hospitalisation. One could say that their life in hospital had become their illness.

Joshua Bierer had introduced these patients into a completely different and more normal environment and found that quite a few could be "resocialised" and guided into a more or less normal life.

Dr E and his companions, with a starting capital of 200 guilders (at present £57) and the help of a philanthropic businessman in Amsterdam, Caransa, had rented a hotel in Zandvoort on the North Sea coast. There they were going to repeat Bierer's experiment, with the nursing staff posing as hotel personnel.

Every client was to have his own private room, could eat in a nice dining-room overlooking the sea, and taste the freedom of normal life again.

Dr E asked me to become the chairman of the board of the Joshua Bierer Foundation.

I told him that I knew next to nothing about psychiatric hospitals, disguised or otherwise, and that I was no better than an idiot when it came to money, my wife firmly governing the financial side of our household.

He assured me that all these things had been taken care of. The only thing he needed was someone he could trust.

As, during the seventies, there was political unrest here and there around psychiatric hospitals, I understood what he meant and took the chairmanship.

In September 1970 everything was ready. I took no part whatsoever in the preparations and had seen the hotel only once. The opening was going to take place on 16 September 1970. My wife and I, dressed like important personages, went to Zandvoort.

It was a strange experience.

I was interviewed by Dutch TV and I gave a talk straight off the cuff, inadvertently stepping on several sensitive toes, as I later heard.

The room where the reception was held was filled to the brim with officials like the mayor of Zandvoort, representatives from the health departments both of Haarlem and at state level, the Hague. There was even a Professor in Psychiatry from the University of Leyden, the great Bastiaans, who had done so much for the rehabilitation of war victims.

One speaker after another climbed the platform and began to shower praises on my head for this initiative and for everything I had done at such short notice in order to set in motion this unique project.

I had of course done nothing at all but I accepted the many praises with a modest smile.

After the official opening many people milled around me and asked a string of difficult questions. One of the hardest ones was: "Who is paying for all this? The AWBZ?"

As I suffer from a slight mental block concerning abbreviations I hadn't a clue what they were talking about but, happily, the new director of the Strand Hotel was hovering in the background, acting as prompt and preventing me from making too many glaring blunders.

When I saw my chance I escaped with my wife to a lift, to "inspect the rest of the hotel". While slowly ascending in this secluded place I asked her, "Is this really happening or is it some dream?"

"Well," she said, "it is rather peculiar, isn't it?"

The celebration dinner that evening, however, was so magnificent that it restored much of my stability.

Right from the start the project was a huge success. After a couple of years we were even able to buy the Strand Hotel and had to rent a second hotel to cope with all the clients. Many of them could be slipped back into a normal life. The Joshua Bierer Foundation became a sort of example for the rest of our country, where other people were now also setting up similar projects, though ours remained by far the largest one.

In 1979 our two accountants advised us to buy the second hotel because in the long run this would be cheaper. We proceeded to act on this advice.

In 1980 a reshuffle took place in the Hague. Up till now we had been subject to the Department of Health and our relationship had always been excellent, but now we became subject to the Department of Culture, Recreation and Society (in Dutch CRM). This proved disastrous.

Our prices in the hotels, where people really were as happy as could be in such circumstances, were one-third of those in the psychiatric hospitals where they came from. The daily tariff was f.71 (this is £20 at today's exchange rate in 1997).

Costs however were slowly increasing. One of our difficulties was that the hotels were situated on the coast, which meant an extraordinary amount of painting to do.

We made a careful calculation and asked CRM for a small rise of 3 guilders a day per patient (85 pence), making the sum total per patient f.74 (£21), which was still extremely low considering how much their residence in a psychiatric hospital would have cost the State.

It was as if CRM had been waiting for their cue. They immediately lowered our price to f.49.51 a day (£14) and bankruptcy stared us in the face. Their argument was, "We did not give you permission to buy the second hotel."

They could not have, of course, as at the time we had bought that hotel we had still been comfortably sheltering under the wings of the Department of Health, but logic is not one of the strong points in the Hague. Our objections were brushed away. So we went with a delegation to the Department of CRM to meet the official who was responsible for this catastrophe. As soon as I was confronted with this man (who had surrounded himself with an enormous staff) I knew that something was seriously wrong. He radiated enmity and he gave me the shivers.

This "Mr NKvD" (not his real initials!) told us that he could not care less if we went bankrupt, as he had never asked us to set up this project in the first place. It became apparent, moreover, that he was set on destroying not only the Joshua Bierer Foundation, but also the members of the board. He wanted to make us personally responsible for the disaster he was causing and bankrupt us individually. We were left with only one thing to do: we brought a lawsuit against the Department of Health.

Slowly, as time progressed, an extremely strange fact emerged. This Mr vD, whom I had only met that one time at his office as part of a delegation, had a wild, personal hatred against me and was bent on destroying me. It was as if the whole attack on the Joshua Bierer Foundation was only a pretext to get at me. Several serious negotiators on our behalf, top men in the health services (Professor Bastiaans being one of them), commented on this incomprehensible fact and asked me what in heaven's name I had done to vD to merit such blind hatred.

The fact that the attack on the Joshua Bierer Foundation was not the prime motive also came out when vD admitted to one of the negotiators in a private conversation that, financially speaking, the buying of the second hotel had been quite a sound move, but that he would play the game by the book. He remained adamant and wanted my head.

So we had to fight for the survival of the Joshua Bierer Foundation and also for our own survival. 120 patients, 60 employees and 5 members of the board had to fight for their existence.

Right at the beginning and during the ensuing court cases, we had an unbelievable piece of luck. We acquired a lawyer, Mr Houthoff, who fought for us like a lion. He was a man who was worth his weight in gold, and while the Joshua Bierer Foundation quietly worked, on its frozen funding, Houthoff fought the Department as David fought Goliath.

I must say that, during the years when all this was happening, I sometimes felt slightly wobbly at the knees. What if we lost our case? I had two children still in the midst of their studies. What if I went bankrupt?

Then, on 6 April 1984 at 3.30 p.m., there was a telephone call from Mr Houthoff. He told me that we had won a complete victory over the Department of CRM and that they now owed us so much money that we could pay all our creditors and still be left with a tidy surplus into the bargain for extra painting, etc.

Here at last comes the coincidence this whole story has been leading up to.

At the exact moment when I was flooded with relief and a weight was lifted from my mind, the telephone still in my hand, out on the square where I live an old-fashioned barrel-organ (we still have them in Holland) burst into peals of joyful music.

We have in Holland a song that is always sung at birthday celebrations and other memorable occasions, a bit like the English "For he's a jolly good fellow". It is called "Long shall they live!" It was this song that burst out of the barrel-organ at the moment I stood there, full of gratitude that the nightmare was over.

I later on discovered that a family living two houses away had hired the organ for a birthday party.

A barrel-organ comes to our square less than once a year and I had never heard one play "Long shall they live". The chances of such a thing happening on that particular day at that specific minute were astronomically small.

The reader might well ask, "What did vD have against you?"

I remember Dave Allen telling a bloodcurdling story on TV about vanishing brides and then, just as he was about to tell you what had happened to the poor women, saying that he never found out.

I never found out why vD hated me in such a personal way, but I will not leave you with the Dave Allen anti-climax. I have a theory but no more than that.

It is not generally recognised how grim the fight for world hegemony has been. After the Second World War the Communist bloc was all for making the whole world communist. This was no secret, it could clearly be read in their own literature.

One of the ways to secure this final victory was the "march through the organs", as it was called. This strange expression described the way in which communist-trained agents became state-officials in countries that had not yet succumbed to communism and slowly climbed up through the ranks, gaining more and more influence over decisions favourable to the final victory.

Another way was to weaken resistance. As much of this resistance could be expected from active Christian organisations, infiltration into those organisations was of paramount importance.

The communists worked in a completely different way from the Nazis. The Nazis used continuous propaganda, a battering from without. I once compared it to a bacterial onslaught.

The communists had a great disdain for such unsubtle methods. They worked their way into groups and tried to manipulate other people into working towards their goals, without revealing those ultimate goals save to some initiates.

"Useful idiots" Lenin had called those who worked for the infiltrators without realising what they were doing. Thus the communist attack could better be compared to an infection by a virus. A virus creeps into a cell and forces it to make another virus similar to itself. The communist attack on the targeted countries came from within.

Another way to effect their aims was by weakening the moral fibre of the youth. There existed a secret communist manual for psychological warfare which taught the political agents how to manipulate the youth of a democratic country. I quote: "By making all sorts of drugs easily available, by giving the teenager alcohol, by praising his rashness, by exciting him with sex magazines or by suggesting to him the sexual practices as described in Sexpol, the psycho-political agent can cultivate the necessary spirit of chaos and unemployment and the feeling of worthlessness, under which circumstances it will be fairly easy to offer the teenager the solution – total freedom under communism."

In the Netherlands we had an organisation called the Dutch Christian Student Association (Dutch initials "NCSV"). In my youth I had been an active member of this Association. University students took part in summer camps, together with high school pupils. During the day they had all sorts of sports and in the evening there were serious talks about the Christian faith and Bible study.

Many youngsters became life-long Christians in those camps. Moreover many people who, later in life, occupied important positions had this Protestant Christian background. We knew each other from NCSV and student days. It was the ideal target for attack.

In the late sixties this NCSV had been secretly infiltrated by trained communists. Early in the seventies the whole top layer of the organisation was communist. Parents sending their children to what they thought were the old, trusted summer camps were bewildered when the children came home with something quite other than Christianity in their heads, but as the attack came "from within", they did not know what to do and moreover they were not organised.

Rumours, but no more than that, about this state of affairs had reached me and after some deliberation my eldest son infiltrated the NCSV. When he came home from their headquarters in Woudschoten he confirmed our worst suspicions.

The Bible had been discarded and in its stead the students were asked to study Marx, Lenin, Mao and Che Guevara. They were also taught that free sexual relationships and soft drugs were to be encouraged.

In the early seventies, half of the students, who in their turn were to influence high school pupils, were already in the power of these new doctrines. The new masters were so sure of themselves that the big white chief had painted a hammer and sickle on top of his car.

Our great problem was how to reach the parents of the high school children, who were dispersed throughout our country.

I mused on the mentality of our enemies and the communist manual and hit upon a plan. On very official-looking paper I wrote a letter to the junta in Woudschoten. I introduced myself as a medical doctor employed at the Academic Hospital in Leyden. I said that we had formed a group for education about drugs. Our aim was to make parents less fearful of the totally harmless soft drugs and let their children experiment with them whenever they wanted. I phrased the letter in the communist jargon I had by now studied thoroughly. At the end I asked the junta to send me their directory with all the addresses of the parents who received annual invitations to send their children to the summer camps. I asked them to send the directory to the porter of the Academic Hospital and signed with a fancy name.

Within a week all the addresses in the Netherlands were in our hands. A friend of mine had simply walked into the porter's lodge and asked, "Has a packet arrived for . . . ?", giving the name with which I had signed. They had swallowed the bait hook, line and sinker.

We then wrote a letter to all the parents in which we explained what had happened to their NCSV. We enumerated all the facts we had discovered and so the whole can of worms was opened. On

13 September *The Telegraph*, our largest daily paper, carried the story as front-page news and my eldest son and I appeared on TV, explaining what had happened to the NCSV.

More facts began to emerge, for instance, that the well-known farm in Uitwellingerga, where summer camps were always held, had been used for intensive communist training of the new staff.

In the meantime the junta still did not understand what had hit them. They could not grasp that we had studied their methods and turned them against them. In two months' time a secret that had been kept since 1967 had become known to everyone. The parents withdrew their support from the NCSV and sent their children to other Christian camps but although any other organisation would have faced immediate bankruptcy, the NCSV was still in existence the following year. A little bird had whispered to me that bankruptcy had been staved off for the time being by a substantial grant from a governmental department in the Hague.

Miscellaneous events and coincidence

Looking at the dates one can see that I became chairman of the Joshua Bierer Foundation in 1970 and that exactly one year later I played a decisive role in disrupting this communist conspiracy.

Had I made a mighty enemy somewhere in a department? Had I stirred up a "sleeper" or a "mule" in his deep cover? Was this the man who made the grant?

There is a certain symmetry in all the events:

– My activities had brought the NCSV to the brink of bankruptcy and they had received help from a department.

– This happened one year after I became chairman of the Joshua Bierer Foundation.

– An official from CRM tried his utmost to wreck our Joshua Bierer Foundation and was bent on my bankruptcy, without knowing me personally.

– This happened as soon as he assumed power over us through a reshuffle of departments.

– I do not say that the hypothetical sleeper and Mr van D who tried to wreck the Joshua Bierer Foundation were one and the same person. The one could have been a friend of the other and asked an unsuspecting vD to destroy me for quite another reason, such as my campaign against fluoridation.

However this may be, according to Occam's law, the explanation of vD's teeth-gnashing enmity against me could be the NCSV adventure. It is a pity I shall not know the truth but I shall never forget that leaden load being lifted from my shoulders and the barrel-organ bursting into its celebration song.

There is something strange about coincidences. As soon as one becomes alert to their existence they begin to multiply.

I am a member of a group consisting of medical doctors, nurses and doctors' assistants. We meet about once every two months in a beautiful convent near Bavel, a village in the southern part of the Netherlands, which is convenient for our Flemish members.

There are always three subjects at our meetings – a medical, a psychological and an ideological or spiritual one.

On 26 October 1996 we decided to dedicate the last hour of our meeting to coincidences happening in our lives. We were asked to be alert to them till the next meeting on 14 December.

Straightaway the phenomenon began to cluster in my life. While usually I note down two or three coincidences a year, during that seven-week period, 11 coincidences happened. Several of them have already been mentioned in this book but here are some more of that cluster.

We have in Holland a very old festival, which has been celebrated for centuries. The famous painter Jan Steen (1626–1679) did a beautiful painting of a Dutch family celebrating this typical family festival.

It is called "Sinterklaas" and when Dutch emigrants landed near the place where New York now stands, they took the festival with them and "Sinterklaas" evolved into "Santa Claus". This American Santa Claus is a rather different figure to our Sinterklaas.

It is celebrated on 5 December. St Nicolas (his official name) appears in the streets as a white-bearded bishop riding a white horse.

He arrives by boat from Spain, as every child knows, and returns there on 6 December. The boats with the bishops can usually be seen on our canals around the time of the celebrations.

He is always attended by one or more black servants, called Black Peters, who are full of mischievous pranks and also carry a bunch of closely-tied branches to spank naughty children with (which of course never happens). Over their shoulders is flung a big bag full of presents, which can also be used to take naughty children back to Spain.

As soon as he arrives in November small children put their shoes near the fireplace (rather difficult today with all the central heating) before going to sleep. They sing some of the age-old songs connected with the feast and the following morning they find a present in their shoes.

What is also known to every child is the way these presents arrive. St Nicolas rides the roofs on his white horse, and stops at each chimney while Peter throws down the presents.

My good mother thought this story an insult to my intelligence. It was clear that the present would burn in the fire before it reached me, so she told me the prosaic story that St Nicolas late at night rang the bell and brought the present in, just like the milkman.

The Feast of St Nicolas is very old indeed. It is a memory of the old heathen god, Odin, riding the clouds on his great white horse, the fearful hunter-magician who ruled over life and death. When the Christian church became dominant in our parts, he was Christianized and changed into the mild and child-loving bishop Nicolas of Myra and his dark heathen and mischievous side was repressed, but not quite because from then on it appeared in the shape of his black servant, who ever accompanied him.

Children love Peter. He is exciting, a little bit of a rascal, never solemn like the good old bishop. The holy Saint has, of course, discarded sexuality altogether (while Odin was a lusty fellow) but one cannot repress reality entirely and that is why Peter carries rod and bag.

St Nicolas, Sinterklaas, is not only a children's festival, far from it. On the evening of 5 December the real feast is celebrated.

Families coming together do things they won't do for the rest of the year. Suddenly every Dutchman has turned into a poet and should one happen to be in a bus or train on the morning of the fifth, one might well see people staring out of the window with a vacant look and then suddenly grabbing a pencil and a piece of paper to write down one more line of the poem they have been brooding on.

Often these poems are funny or carry an educational message or refer to something that happened the previous year.

Apart from that there are so-called "surprises". The many presents we give each other are made to look like something else. I suspect this part of the festivities to have been borrowed from the Jewish Purim festival where they do a similar thing. In these surprises the full ingenuity of those who still celebrate St Nicholas in the old-fashioned way is employed. There is a ring at the front door and a life-size figure of a man with a strange mask stares at the astonished children, causing delightful shivers down their spines. When the man is dismantled the presents are revealed.

Another time the children have to dip their hands into a bucket full of extremely dirty-looking water to find what they seek. There are cardboard houses, mysteriously lighted grottos in the cellar. Everything one can dream up is secretly constructed during the weeks preceding the festival. Rooms are out of bounds, an atmosphere of delightful expectation pervades the house.

Those engrossed in the noble work derive at least as much pleasure from their surprises as those on the receiving end.

Often, just like in the poems, the surprises remind the receiver of something that has happened to him or her during the previous year, preferably something stupid or ridiculous.

The average St Nicolas fan looks down his nose at the mere Santa Clauses appearing in our shops at Christmas nowadays after the American example. We, the old-fashioned Sinterklaas revellers, consider them imposters.

The phenomenon of coincidence loves to be present when people become creative as the following examples will show.

On Friday evening, 15 November 1996, at 5.30 p.m. I was busy making a "surprise" for one of my grandsons, Ewoud, aged ten.

In the Netherlands we have a children's game called "Stap op" ("Get on your bike"). It consists of cards with pictures on, many of them depicting handicaps for those on a bicycle, like an adverse wind, a burst tyre or close barriers at a railway crossing.

I made for Ewoud an alternative game, in which he had to ride home from school on his bike, in time for lunch, and was distracted by all sorts of things happening on the road.

The picture I was drawing at that particular moment on Friday afternoon was related to a memory from my youth.

In Amsterdam many shops would hire men to dress up as St Nicolas to liven up business. Once, at the end of November, a magnificent St Nicolas on a white horse was riding proudly through a narrow street when, from the other side, there approached another splendid St Nicolas on a white horse., much to the confusion of the children under six, who still believed in the one and only children's friend.

Now it so happened that both these riders considered this street as their private domain. When they met they first exchanged the sort of words that should never pass the lips of a saint and then an appalling fight broke out. The two holy men bashed each other wherever they could with their brightly-gilded staffs, much to the glee of the assembled public, who encouraged the contestants with loud cries.

At last the police arrived and arrested the two by now rather dishevelled bishops for disrupting public order.

A month later, reduced to their proper size in their sober daily attire, they stood on trial. They confessed that in their capacity as St Nicolas they had let themselves go a bit too far. My father, the

Public Prosecutor, was so amused by the whole story that he imposed a very small fine indeed.

Remembering this incident I drew a picture of two fighting St Nicolas figures on horses, beating each other with their staffs.

My eldest son, Ewoud's father, hearing what I was doing, warned me that Wessel, the youngest son, was still a devout believer and he asked me to make it clear in the "surprise" that one of the figures was a fake St Nicolas. So I blurred one of them a bit and moreover made it clear in the poem accompanying the picture that only one of the St Nicolas figures represented the real one.

That evening I finished the card of the two fighting men to my satisfaction. The next morning, Saturday 16 November, I opened the daily paper and to my utter astonishment one of the first things I saw was a large coloured photo of a real St Nicolas and a Santa Claus (to our eyes, a fake one), straddling a tiled roof, as if they were on horseback. They were confronting each other and hitting each other with their gilded staffs. Even that little detail of one real and one fake St Nicolas tallied with the card I had drawn the previous evening.

Miscellaneous events and coincidence

The next day, 17 November 1997, my wife and I made a "surprise" for Sarie, my eldest grandchild, then aged 12.

My wife had bought a new cassette tape and we were going to make a sort of radio play. The subject was Dracula.

One hears a lonely traveller on his horse (clip clop clip clop) in the Carpathian mountains. It is a windy evening (sound of wind) and the rider approaches a dark castle. When he finally arrived he dismounts and knocks at the door.

Slowly, with a creaking sound, it opens and a high, whining voice asks, "Who is there?"

The traveller then asks (in my voice) if he can stay the night and he is let inside. The servant is heard quickly grabbing a cockroach and making a crunching noise as he eats it.

Then a cellar door opens and a solemn, deep voice (me at my lowest octave) asks, "Who is there?"

"I am a lonely traveller," my voice says. "I cannot travel any farther tonight. Could I stay here if it is not inconvenient to you?"

"I am Count Dracula," says the solemn voice. "You are welcome to stay here and my servant will give you dinner. Your horse shall be stabled. I myself will not join you for dinner as I will have it upstairs in my own room."

One hears Count Dracula ascending the stairs and a moment later a heartrending cry.

It would seem he is sucking blood from a young maiden.

Then follows a talk between the traveller and the servant and some more adventures in which coffins in a cellar play an important role.

When we had finished the whole sinister story, we played back the tape to satisfy ourselves that everything was all right.

A real surprise awaited us. There appeared to be a flaw in the new tape. Everything went well until the cellar door opened, but at the moment Count Dracula opens his mouth the sound changes and the voice echoes as it would in a deep, spacious cellar. Then my "normal" voice is heard, but it does not sound normal any more. It wavers and trembles as if the traveller is mortally afraid. Again the solemn, echoing voice speaks and once more the traveller's trembling voice is heard.

Then Count Dracula vanishes and when the traveller talks to the servant everything is back to normal and stays that way for the rest of the tape.

I played the whole tape for my group on 14 December, when we had to report our coincidences and everyone agreed that this was a clear case of a most remarkable coincidence. The tape was moreover far better than my wife and I could have managed on our own.

The last example makes it clear that the phenomenon sometimes gives you just the right help at the moment you need it.

About once a week my assistant, who can hardly cope with all the work, is assisted in her turn by another nurse, who normally works in a convent for elderly nuns nearby.

I had to make a "surprise" for this Loes, but she is such a sweet person, and she is so compliant and unimpeachable that I could not find a suitable subject to pull her leg about.

On 19 November at 8.30 a.m. I stepped into my assistant's room and there I also found Loes, who had just returned from her night-shift in the convent and was leaning against a table in a state of near-exhaustion.

The very first thing I heard her say was, "I could have murdered that nun! I could have killed her!"

It appeared that a decrepit and mentally rather disturbed elderly nun had called her that night at least sixteen times for nothing.

So of course I silently thanked my stars and that evening faked a daily paper which ran on the front page a story about sweet old Sister Innocentia being brutally murdered by a nurse, L from H. One sees pictures of Sister Innocentia in happier days talking with the Pope, and of Loes with a black bar over her eyes, the same devise used by the papers when a picture of some convicted gangster enlivens a bloodcurdling article.

We will end this chapter with a romantic story.

Early in 1981 I took my usual twenty-minute walk through the woods nearby, "Haarlem Wood". It is quite famous in our history and was extensively described in the 19th century by one of our celebrated writers, Hildebrand. His "unpleasant man in Haarlem Wood" has become an expression. His statue can be seen in the wood, overlooking a fountain surrounded by all the people he created in his book *Camera Obscura*. The book was obligatory reading in our schools, or at least was when my wife and I were at school. Nowadays with tradition being a dirty word I am not so sure.

While I was walking on that beautiful morning in spring, I suddenly noticed a young couple. He was carving something in the bark of an enormous beech tree and she, standing with her back towards me, looked on admiringly, leaning forward a little so as not to miss anything.

The next day I saw what had been carved – a heart and the names Judith and Arthur. Also the date "4.4.'81".

For a couple of years I would regularly pass the tree with their names on it and the couple acquired a warm place in my heart.

Then one day I saw to my sorrow that someone had interfered with some of the letters, giving them some nasty scratches. I began to fret about the beloved couple and at last I wrote a letter to the local paper (*Haarlems Dagblad*) asking, "Judith and Arthur, where are you? Your names carved in the tree have become for me like a homely scar on a beloved face. Have you split up or has some vandal desecrated this memory?"

The daily paper lapped it up and printed an article under the title "Judith and Arthur, where are you?", complete with a picture of the tree.

This article was published on 5 December 1983.

On the evening of 9 December there was a ring at the front door. My wife opened it and I heard people being led into the waiting-room.

"People for you," she said, and there was secret laughter in her eyes.

I entered the waiting-room and found a young couple there. A nice, sturdy young man and a young woman who had been in my practice since she was a toddler, Judith H.

She got up, shook my hand, laughed and said, "Doc, whatever have you been doing? Making fun of me?"

At first, I did not understand her question, but then it slowly dawned on me that this must be the girl I had seen nearly three years ago and not recognised because she had been standing with her back to me. So this young man must be Arthur and they were obviously still together.

We all had a good laugh and the local paper had a field day publishing the happy ending with a picture of the couple.

On 23 December 1985 another picture appeared of them, now bride and bridegroom, with yours truly congratulating them. The local paper had followed the story right up to the wedding.

When, in 1984, Haarlem celebrated the 400th birthday of its wood, the romantic interlude I have just described was mentioned in the memorial book and the tall beech has ever since then been called the "Moolenburgh Tree".

By the way, the original woods are much older, being part of a far larger forest that covered most of our country in ancient times (Holland means "Woodland") but during the siege of Haarlem (1571–1573), the wood was cut down by Spanish troops to get a clear field of fire for their guns pounding the city-walls. A lane half-a-mile from where I live is still called "Spaniards' Lane" as it was there that the guns were positioned.

Was the story of Judith and Arthur a coincidence? Certainly.

The chance that I just happened to walk along during the short time Arthur was carving their names in the bark (the only reason why the names had become dear to me) combined with the chance that this was one of my own dear patients, whom I had known from childhood and whose young love was immortalized in the bark of that tree, resulted in a typical coincidence, relating in a meaningful way two seemingly unconnected facts.

DOES THE LAW of coincidence – as by now we might call the phenomenon – play a role in the Bible?

Certainly, when we know where to look for it.

Time and again, both in the Old and in the New Testament, we are told that people "cast lots" to come to a decision. More or less as the Chinese did with their *I Ching*.

89 times, 78 in the Old and 11 in the New Testament, lots are cast in all sorts of situations.

In 19 Old Testament books and in 5 New Testament books (all four Gospels and Acts) the practice is mentioned.

11

5th Intermezzo
The Bible and coincidence

The first time we find it is in Leviticus 16:8, when on the great day of atonement the High Priest Aaron had to choose the goat which was going to bear the sins of the people away into the desert, The Lord Himself orders Moses to make the choice in this way.

The last time the Bible mentions the casting of lots is in Acts 1:26, when a new apostle must be chosen instead of Judas who betrayed Jesus and afterwards committed suicide.

Apparently, casting lots was a perfectly legitimate way of taking decisions and the results were considered an act of God, as we can read in the above-mentioned extract from Acts: "Please," the disciples pray "show us, Lord, who knows all hearts the one that you from the two have chosen . . . " (there were two candidates). Then they do not wait for His voice but cast lots and consider the result as His answer.

In Isaiah 34:17 it is even written that the Lord Himself casts lots to decide where all sorts of animals (mentioned in the previous verses) will live in the desolation after the destruction of Edom. Apparently Einstein's remark that God doesn't play dice needs some fresh consideration.

That the Lord is indeed actually engaged in the lot-casting business we can see from a story told in Joshua 6 and 7.

After 40 years of exile in the desert Israel at last entered the promised land and began to conquer Canaan. They were, during this conquest, expressly forbidden to take any spoils.

One of the reasons behind this prohibition might have been that the inhabitants of Canaan were riddled with nasty idolatrous habits, like burning their first-born children alive in a huge red-hot idol of the god Baal to ensure a good harvest. There were a lot of unpleasant goings-on and Joshua probably wanted to protect his people from acquiring ritual objects connected with these horrors, as negative acts can be infectious.

A certain Mr Achan ignored the command and pinched a beautiful coat and a considerable amount of gold and silver and hid the loot in his tent.

Straightaway an enemy battalion defeated the – up till then – victorious Israeli army.

Joshua immediately asked the Lord why this had happened and received the answer, "Because they touched forbidden goods."

Observe that the Lord did not say, "That rascal Achan has grabbed some loot, which he should not have done."

The Lord only mentions the sort of crime that had been perpetrated and then proceeds by giving exact instructions: the whole of Israel must assemble and establish the guilty party by process of elimination.

We do not know exactly how this was done, but we do know for sure that it was not a police investigation by means of interrogation.

Using a procedure more related to the *I Ching* than to the little grey cells of Hercule Poirot, the culprit's hiding-place is pinpointed. This is done by casting lots.

First the guilty tribe is found, in this case, Judah.

Then the guilty clan, in this case, Zerah.

Then the guilty family, in this case, Zabdi.

Finally, the guilty man, Achan.

He confesses, the loot is found, there is no psychiatrist to tell the judge that social inequality made him act the way he did, and he is executed.

It would appear that this game of chance worked to perfection and was absolutely legal, as the Lord Himself had ordered it.

Why the Lord chose to find Achan in such a roundabout fashion is not told. A possible explanation might be that doing it like this involved the whole people in an intensely emotional way and had great educational value.

This way, the people could not simply shrug it off with, "That Achan again. I told you the chap was no good."

No, there must have been deep anxiety.

First in the whole of Israel. A searching of hearts must have taken place. Many a man would have thought back to the beautiful things he had nearly pilfered.

Then, when the tribe of Judah was singled out, there would have been shame in that tribe and great commiseration expressed by the other tribes who would also have felt secretly guilty because of their relief that the crime had not fallen to their lot, while Judah was in trouble.

Had they known Bunyan they would have thought, "There but for the grace of God go we".

Slowly and inexorably the anxiety must have mounted as the game of chance went on, narrowing the field of suspects, and at last pinpointing the culprit. Each time, this process of anxiety, relief, shame, guilt and commiseration must have repeated itself.

The amount of empathy generated must have been enormous.

There would be no more looting in future. The lesson had been taken to heart.

What was the technique of casting lots? It is not quite clear, but in the above case the Jewish commentaries say that the famous Urim and Thummim played roles. They were the two great crystals in the breastplate of the High Priest, described in Exodus 28:30.

Some say that when the High Priest asked a question of the Lord and the answer was "yes", the Urim would light up and when the answer was "no", the Thummim would light up.

But finding answers was not always done like this. When Aaron had to choose the goat for the desert he put his hand into an urn and simply drew out a lot.

When the new land of Israel is divided among the tribes, the Lord orders it to be done by lot. Again the manner is not specified. Several methods were probably used, for instance, tossing coins as in the *I Ching*.

That the method was widespread among heathen populations also we can see from the story of Jonah.

The Lord said to Jonah, "Go to Nineveh, that big city and tell her that her sins have come up before me."

This meant that Nineveh, just like Sodom and Gomorrah, would be destroyed.

What does Jonah do? He goes hell for leather not to the east, towards Nineveh, but westwards, to the coast, and embarks on a ship which is sailing for Tarsus, far across the Mediterranean.

Why did he do this?

Nineveh was the capital city of the Assyrian empire which threatened the North Kingdom, Israel, with total annihilation.

I often wondered what I would have done in a similar situation.

Say it is 1939.

My father was connected with counter-espionage and from 1936 on I had heard him talk about a possible attack on the West by a fast-growing German military power.

I remember a day in 1939 when German soldiers were reported to be approaching our frontier. Only a few knew this but in Dutch military circles the alarm had been given. That evening Father paced like a caged tiger to and fro in the house. At the last moment the army swerved aside. Was it a postponed attack? An exercise? We never knew what it was. The real attack came on 10 May 1940.

What I have been wondering is this:–

Imagine that I had suddenly heard the Lord's voice saying to me, "Go to Berlin, that big city, and tell her that her sins have come up before me."

I would have told my father and if he had believed me he probably would have said, "Listen, there is just a chance that these Nazis might do what the men in Nineveh did: they'll pull a pious face and go through a sort of conversion. Do you think it will last? Forget it. They will only lie low for one or two years and then try again to conquer the whole of Western Europe [that the Nazis would go much farther than that did not even occur to us]. So let them be destroyed. Good riddance. Flee to London and hide there for a short time until Berlin has vanished from the face of the earth. Let us keep this strictly between us."

I do not know what I would have done but the chances are that I would have obeyed my earthly father rather than my heavenly one.

Had a talk like this taken place between Jonah and his father, Amittai? We know that Jonah fled west instead of east, just as I probably would have done. He took the boat from Joppa, nowadays the quaint little town of Jaffa just south of Tel Aviv. Then, when they were at sea, there came a terrific storm which threatened to destroy the ship.

Nowadays we would have thought it was caused by a meteorological depression, but in those enlightened days the sailors asked themselves if the storm might have come on purpose. Jewish commentaries moreover say that the storm was extremely localised. The sailors could see other ships in the not too far off distance having no trouble at all. Perhaps this strange state of affairs set them thinking.

Anyhow there is Jonah, sleeping down below, not minding the storm.

One is struck by the parallel with Christ sleeping in a boat while the storm is raging on the lake and the disciples are afraid for their lives.

In essence it is the same story. As a matter of fact every word in the story of Jonah (as in the rest of the Bible) has several layers of higher meanings. I will only concern myself here with the historical narrative.

The ship's mate awakens Jonah and then the sailors cast lots to discover which of them is the cause of their dangerous situation. It is Jonah.

At first, the sailors try to save him, for they are really nice men, but when it becomes clear that they are heading for disaster Jonah begs them to throw him overboard.

We know how later on he is saved by a big fish and ends up in Nineveh. He warns the city, a real conversion takes place, and Jonah is extremely vexed with the Lord when the destruction he has foretold does not happen.

He had ample reason for his anger since it was the Assyrians who eventually drove Israel into an exile from which they never returned.

One of the amazing points in this story is that the casting of lots by a heathen crew was instrumental in bringing Jonah to Nineveh and in the Lord's will being done.

Again we see that mysterious link between God and coincidence. For isn't tossing a coin, or throwing a dice, or whatever, pure chance to the logical mind?

Then how can God, the great Law-giver in the Universe, be linked to such an erratic phenomenon as coincidence? Isn't that a first-class mystery? Are we wrong about coincidence or about the nature of God or what? Let us analyse the idea of coincidence a bit more as it occurs in the Old Testament.

The word generally used all through the Old Testament for lot is "goral". It is drawing lots, letting chance decide, trusting that this action on earth will coincide with God's will, all rolled into one.

Weinreb said, "Drawing lots is a non-logical answer to a question."

In Hebrew there exists a technique for discovering which words are closely related. It is by counting numerical values.

Nowadays we have a similar procedure in DNA analysis. DNA spirals are ordered like an alphabet and with the help of that code we can find closely-related species, even if their outward appearances might be quite different.

When two words have an identical numerical value they are closely related, even if their superficial meaning seems to be completely different.

The numerical value of the word goral = 3-300-20 = 233 which is the same as the word for foot, "regel" = 300-3-20 = 233.

In this case one can even say that regel (vowels not included) is an anagram of goral.

What is the connection between a foot and chance?

For us in the 20th century it is extremely difficult to understand. Nowadays we think we know exactly where we are going. We walk on this earth with great arrogance. Yet ancient knowledge has it that we are not the movers but the moved. A creative invisible background weaves us into a pattern which we do not understand and call "chance" or "coincidence", but there is structure in it.

In Holland we had a famous clairvoyant who often helped the police to find missing persons (Croiset).

When this man was asked to describe all the people in the first row of a theatre, where he was due to give a performance a fortnight later, he did so. His descriptions proved accurate, despite the fact that there were people who had only bought a ticket that very evening or received a ticket from people who suddenly could not go.

We have a feeling that we could change our lives at any moment but that is an illusion. Stepping out of the pattern into a new one requires a special effort. There is a beautiful story to illustrate that point, told me one night by my Hebrew teacher:

Once, long ago, there was a group of labourers clearing rocks from a piece of land. It was hard work and when, at noon, the sun would blaze down intensely (it happened in the Middle East), they would sit down in the shadow of a high rock wall. Then the boss would go round with a basket and each labourer would drop into it the food he had brought. Some had bread, another fruit, a third cheese, etc. One day, when the boss was engaged in this task, he came to a man who had no food with him. His wife was ill and he had given all his money to the doctor. The man hung his head and was very ashamed, but the boss shielded him from the others, made as if to help the man throw something particularly heavy into the basket, and said, "Well, you *are* spoiling us today", thus saving the face of the poor man. The boss walked along the row but it had taken him just a few moment longer than usual to reach his usual spot because of the extra attention he had given this poor man. Two steps before he reached his place a large piece of rock suddenly broke off and hit the place where the boss always sat. It would have squashed him to jelly if he had not spared the unfortunate labourer that extra time.

"That piece of rock," say the commentaries, "had waited there from the beginning of creation to kill the boss. But as he went out of his way to do something good not expected from him, his fate changed and he stayed alive."

The moral of the Hebrew tale is that "doing good saves you from death".

The second word or, rather, words with the same numerical value as goral is the "Tree of Life", in Hebrew "Ets Hachaim". The numerical value is 70-90 5-8-10-10-40 = 233.

This tree, which is mentioned both at the very beginning of the

Bible in Genesis 2 and at the very end in Revelation 22, gave eternal life and was the opposite of the tree of the knowledge of good and evil which brought death.

Hebrew lore says that the roots of the two trees were closely intertwined.

This is an indication that, behind this world where death and decay seem to rule supreme, there exists a bubbling and eternal fountain of life.

It cannot be reached by logical analytical thinking, neither by magical techniques. It simply IS, ready to show glimpses of itself as soon as we have acquired a certain measure of humility.

Our intellectual arrogance has nearly destroyed our beautiful planet. Perhaps it is time to become once more conscious of the fact that pursuing materialistic science is to tread the path of death.

Wonder and delight, however, can be the first step on the road towards life. Sometimes small coincidences can be the road signs towards that feeling of joyful astonishment which many people lose when they grow up.

There is one other important example in the Old Testament where the casting of lots is mentioned and we can find it in the book of Esther.

The story takes place in the 5th century before Christ.

In it we are told about a mighty man called Haman. He climbed so high on the social ladder that he was in fact just below the King.

Every dignitary in court prostrated himself before Haman or bent his knee, because to crawl before an exalted man in those (and these) times was the better part of wisdom, especially when a totalitarian king has made it obligatory.

In the palace, there was also a Jew, Mordecai, but he neither prostrated himself before Haman nor bent his knee. Apparently he was not impressed by his upstart and moreover one does not prostrate oneself for anyone but God.

Now this put Haman in a quandary. Personal vengeance was far beneath his dignity and it would also show him up for the spiteful little bastard he really was.

So he concocted a better plan. He discovered that Mordecai was a Jew and decided to annihilate all the Jews. In that way he could get at Mordecai without anyone seeing what he was really doing. On a grand scale he did more or less what Mr NKvD tried to do to the Joshua Bierer Foundation, disguising the fact that he was trying to get at me.

So Haman went to the king and told him that among all the people in Persia only the Jews despised the King's laws; wouldn't it be better to destroy them?

Small psychopaths in high positions are always extremely dangerous, as we have seen with Himmler, Hitler's henchman.

The king assented to this plan, especially after Haman promised him a considerable amount of cash for his treasury.

We are then told that Haman threw the "pur", again translated as "lot", every month and found that on the 13th day of the 12th month all the Jews could be murdered.

Why is not the word goral but pur used here? What is this pur? Is it just another way of letting chance decide?

Weinreb says in his book about Esther that the pur is quite the opposite of chance. Haman works with what he thinks is a watertight scientific system, which one by one eliminates all the months except for one and all the days in that last month except for one.

We do not quite know how this pur worked, but we can make an educated guess. It was probably done with astrology.

Having had a friend who cast a horoscope for every important (and unimportant) decision, I can imagine how it was done.

Haman probably calculated the best time with the help of the – in his age already well developed – celestial chart. In his time it was considered to be a highly accurate and scientific method.

Most people know what happened. Queen Esther, unbeknown to the king a niece of Mordecai, with great courage threw herself into the battle and instead of the Jews all their enemies were destroyed, including Haman and his ten sons.

This fact is still remembered in the Purim celebrations, when the Jews make "surprises" for each other to remind themselves of the complete surprise when all turned out for the best.

Weinreb pointed out a peculiar fact: something must have gone wrong with Haman's calculations. What was it?

Was he a bad astrologer? The explanation is this:–

In Israel a year lasted 360 days. This meant that, just as in our times we have to intercalate a leap day once in four years to keep time with the sun, so Israel had to intercalate a whole month after 6 years, and this was the month Adar, the 12th month.

Haman threw his pur only 12 times in a year with an extra 12th month, a 13th month, and this overthrew the iron laws of the stars and gave the Jews precisely that amount of space, which led to their being saved. Haman was literally out in his reckoning.

Please do not try to understand this explanation in a mathematical sense. It has to do with the meaning and quality of numbers: 12 is the number of the immutable laws of our universe, 13 is the number of freedom.

It is wonderful how this principle of liberty, that crazy 13th month, conquers the iron laws of the Medes and Persians. The freedom hidden in our creation can play havoc with seemingly indomitable laws and make them flexible, not carved in stone at all.

So in the Old Testament we have these two marvellous opposing conceptions of goral and pur, God-given Chance and puny man's calculation.

We often see how people can be saddled with a problem too big for them to handle in a rational and logical way. They try and try but it cannot be solved by normal methods.

In the Old Testament these questions were, for instance:
– Why is Israel losing a battle against a weaker enemy?
– Why is this storm lashing only our ship?
– How are we to divide the land without provoking envy?
In our times we could add a lot more of these questions:
– Why is everyone talking about environmental pollution and why is there not one politician who really does something to stop it?
– Why do we have the technology for clean machines and do not develop it on a grand scale?
– Why do we treat cancer with ever stronger poisons while deaths from it continue to increase? (Notwithstanding regular assurances that now at last there is a real break-through.)
– Why are taxes squandered on crazy plans that won't work?
And so on and so forth.

In Old Testament times, it is at the point when such questions are asked that coincidence steps into the breach. The non-logical, non-linear creative side takes over.

De Bono would undoubtedly call it "lateral thinking". Life, after all, is not logical. Love, the great driving force in life, is not logical. The platypus is not logical. We can relax.

The idea of "utilitarianism" has in our century been a harsh and relentless taskmaster.

We have been so thoroughly indoctrinated with the utilitarianism principle that we cannot understand a lot of very important facts. Animals don't always play because they "must learn how to hunt". They play for fun. It happens to help them later on in their hunting but the grim business of life is not the whole explanation.

Giraffes did not elongate their necks by searching for leaves in the tree-tops (as Lamarck postulated). It is far more probable that they were created because the Creator is always full of fun ideas. Perhaps

139

the platypus is a good joke and the giraffe a surrealistic painting by a superb artist.

All these things are related to goral, to delightful coincidences.

Then, on the other hand, we find the other concept, pur. Man as an economic unit. The survival of the fittest. Dehumanised medical science. "Have you taken a blood sample from the appendix in bed 6?"

Haman, the prototype for a dictator, wants things clean, uniform, on one level. Perhaps one of the best definitions of a dictator is "A man who has no sense of humour".

Dictators never laugh "from the heart". In essence they are not human. They have died long ago. Look at their stony faces, their marionette-like movements.

Yet they who think that they can calculate everything are defeated by that no. 13, the fool, the odd man out. Just a tiny blade of grass can pierce the concrete of a highway. So an insignificant nobody with an original idea can topple a seemingly immovable structure.

The unholy trio of University-State-Industry which forced fluoridation on the Netherlands was brought down by a small group of insignificant people who had one thing in common: they could not be corrupted.

Creation is always stronger than rigidity, it simply sweeps resistance away like an autumnal storm does rotten wood.

The most famous example in the Bible of letting chance decide we find in the New Testament. It was of course the casting of lots by the Roman soldiers for the garments of the crucified Christ.

This event is considered so important that all four Gospels mention it (Matth. 27:35, Mark 15:24, Luke 23:34, John 19:23).

It is the fulfilment of a prophecy made by David in Psalm 22:18.

> "They part my garments among them,
> and cast lots upon my vesture."

If the Old and New Testaments stress this point in no uncertain terms we would do well to analyse this story carefully.

I will quote the story as it is told in John and as literal translation is important for the analysis, I will follow the Concordant Version, where every Greek word is always translated by the same English word. This makes the reading sometimes less easy but you know at least exactly where you are.

"The soldiers then, when they crucify Jesus, took his garments and made four parts, to each soldier a part and the tunic.

Now the tunic was seamless, woven from above throughout the whole.

They said to one another 'We should not be rending it, but we may take chances on it, whose it shall be', that the scripture may be fulfilled which is saying: 'They divide my garments among themselves and on my vesture they cast the lot'.

The soldiers indeed then do these things." (John 19: 23–25)

Why is this story deemed so important that all the gospels have it?

It seems to be a fairly trivial detail with soldiers behaving as they have always done, dividing the spoil.

We must go beyond the literal meaning of the words to understand the message, and not remain with Roman soldiers playing a game of dice 2000 years ago. If that were all there was to it, we might as well forget it. Let us analyse the main elements of the story.

The players are Roman soldiers, servants of the Roman Government.

What is Rome? What does it stand for?

Ancient teaching covers four successive "exiles" in human history.

1. The Babylonian, symbolized in Nebuchadnezzar's dream by the golden head of the great image.
2. The Medo-Persian, represented by silver arms and a silver breast.
3. The greek, pictured as the belly and thighs made of bronze.
4. The Roman, symbolised by legs of iron.

(Daniel 2: 31–3)

They are "exiles" because they symbolise humanity falling deeper and deeper into materialistic concepts, losing more and more of its spirituality and finally forgetting God altogether.

In Babylon there was still a memory of the one and only God In Medi-Persia it began to dim and gold became silver. In Greece human philosophy began to rule supreme. It looked like gold but it was bronze. Finally came the Roman exile in which we are still living, as far removed from God as possible.

In Hebrew tradition Rome was called Edom, the place connected with that strong and worldly man, Esau. We could call Rome a symbol of the world, the exterior world of sensory perception, the opposite of the interior world.

When Jesus, the King of the interior world, the spiritual world, and Pilate, the representative of the exterior world, the Roman world, meet, Jesus says to him loudly and clearly, "My kingdom is not of this world" (John 18:36).

An all-out opportunist like Pilate could not of course understand this.

Another indication that the Roman soldiers represent this world is that there are four of them. Four is the number belonging to the physical world, where everything has four aspects:

The four parts of the day
The four seasons
The four directions of the compass
The four elements
The four historical kingdoms just mentioned (exiles)
The four realms of physical reality – humans, animals, plants, minerals
The four ages of man – youth, adolescence, maturity, old age

What could this division by the world of Jesus' garments mean?

Someone's garments make up his exterior appearance. One could perhaps say that Jesus' garments were his life history, seen in a purely historical sense.

These were taken by the world and used for its own exterior purposes.

During the crusades, for instance, the "Christians" with the cross as their symbol butchered the Jews on their way to the Holy Land and the Arabs in the Holy Land. Thousands died.

"Christians" in the name of their Saviour burned their opponents (fellow Christians but with a different conception of Christianity) at the stake, after torturing them in a horrible way. First the Roman Church, with its Inquisition, but later Calvin who also had his opponents burned.

Half-a-million Cathars and Albigensians were brutally murdered in southern France at the instigation of the Pope.

Let us move to the 20th century.

During World War Two, 3 million Russian and Polish Jews were slaughtered by special police battalions operating in the rear of the front-line soldiers. Daniel Jonah Goldhagen has written in his well-documented book *Hitler's Willing Executioners* that these battalions did not consist entirely of trained young SS men but, for the main part, of mature men, all volunteers, who regularly went home on leave, were family men and went to church as they often came from a Lutheran background.

During the war I did not hear of one church making an official protest against the Holocaust. Many individual Christians helped Jews, and even lost their lives as a result, but I am talking about official Christianity. The church leaders were not unaware of what was happening, they knew.

This is the world, wearing the garments of Christ, using the great Christian symbols, and yet at heart remaining as murderous as it has always been.

Now we come to the tunic. The core of the matter.

The translation "coat" in the King James version of the Bible is wrong.

In Greek it is the word "chiton", a tunic worn next to the body. In Hebrew it is called "ketonet" and the first time it is described in the Old Testament is as one of the garments of a priest.

The King James version again has "broidered coat" (Ex. 28:4), but it is a check tunic, worn next to the skin.

"Undershirt" would perhaps come closest to it.

Weinreb told us that in Hebrew tradition this garment is seen as the symbol of the physical body.

We now come closer to what happened at the foot of the cross.

A sort of game is played around the ketonet, the symbol of the physical body of the Lord, and the prize is carried away by one of the Roman soldiers. It is in my view a great prophecy.

What was the great message of the new Christian faith?

– That God had appointed one single Mediator between Himself and humanity (1 Tim. 2:5)

– That through the death of this Mediator sins were forgiven.

– That those who believed in Him could live in hope of resurrection.

– That the proof of their belief in Him was that they would live a life of charity and forgiveness of others.

– Love was the great message. Not love as it is celebrated on TV nowadays, which is a lower sort of sex, but love which loves without expecting any recompense – the highest form of love.

The early Christians were given the Holy Spirit because under their own steam they could never carry out the commission given to them. In essence Christianity was easy to understand.

Love, compassion, forgiveness, hope, joy, faith – those were the key-words. All went well for a few centuries, but then there was a spiritual catastrophe. In the great heathen centre, Rome, the old paganism was overthrown. A Christian ruler took power and the Christian church became the State Church.

Anything worse could hardly be imagined. The Church, the community of people living according to the precepts of the King of Peace, became a political powerbase.

In the 325th year of our Lord, disaster struck in the shape of the Council of Nicaea.

Emperor Constantine the Great mounted the first real lobbying campaign in world history, a uniform church doctrine was accepted and a spiritual totalitarian rule was initiated.

It would be another 200 years before the State Church ruled supreme, but this was where it all started.

Paul had taught the early Christians that they were the body of Christ. Their Lord was the head, but they were His members on earth, fulfilling His will. Just as the head in the human body sends out directions to the rest of the body and is the seat of the spirit, so Christ, through His Spirit, governed His members on earth, not as a totalitarian ruler, but always lovingly.

As soon as the Church became political, however, an instrument of power and suppression, that was the end of the in-dwelling spirit.

The Spirit was withdrawn.

This is made strikingly obvious when one studies the Council of Nicaea. Up till then the human structure was believed to consist of spirit, soul and body. In Nicaea the dogma was accepted that the human structure consisted of soul and body.

The spirit was thrown out.

What is a human being without his spirit? He is dead.

The Church, the Body of Christ, became the official church, the dead body of Christ. The great prophecy hidden in the Roman soldier's acquisition of the tunic by rolling dice had been fulfilled.

The great message of grace and love was more and more forgotten.

Up till 325 AD the resurrected Christ was the centre of Christian life, but now an enormous cult was built up around the battered body hanging on the cross. Death became more important than life. The State Church had gained by its machinations in the game of Nicaea (where its opponents were gagged) the ketonet, the dead body of Christ, but it had lost the Spirit. Popes, following the example given by Constantine, dressed in purple, the triple crown on their heads, and as history progressed, the Church became ever more cruel in its suppression of those who deviated slightly from the official rules or thoughts.

Mind, I am not talking about "that awful Roman Catholic Church".

I am talking about any official church which gets too closely involved in "the world". When the Protestant faith gained complete victory in Holland after 80 years of war against Spain, Roman Catholics became second-class citizens and it took them more than

200 years to be accepted as equals by the powers that be. So please understand that I am talking about the world trying to annex the inner kingdom and failing. It is rather a sad story.

One more thing should be said about the "ketonet", the tunic.

Weinreb told us that every one of the priests' garments, according to the old teaching, was related to a certain vice. If you had that vice, you were not allowed to wear that garment. The vice connected with the tunic was: "Discovering the secret parts", an expression we find in the Old Testament. What does it mean? In essence it means that the physical body (symbolised by the ketonet) gets the upper hand. A human being is overwhelmed by the world of the senses and forgets that he or she is a spiritual being, too. In our times that vice is extremely active.

Modern science has discovered how vast the universe is and many people nowadays say, "Even our sun is no more than a speck of dust in this vast universe. What then is this earth, what a human being? Nothing at all." They "drown" in space. They forget that mere bigness does not tell us anything about importance.

Such a nihilistic attitude can easily lead to a letting go of all moral values. If nothing is important, why bother? This is "discovering the secret parts".

Another aspect of this vice is teaching that the human being is just another mammal.

The Church has not been able to help in this dilemma because the Church, whatever it may say, is the world. If it were the living body of Christ it could muster enough resistance to ward off the attack of secularised science, but it cannot, because it is the dead body of Christ: His body from the moment He died on the cross to the moment of His resurrection three days later.

I am not talking nonsense. Making a mere mammal, an ape, the ancestor of the human being is teaching false doctrine. One would expect the Church to be the first to come out with good scientific arguments to refute this teaching. But the Church is the world and so we read in october 1996 in the daily papers:

"Pope Recognises Evolution Theory.
Yesterday in a letter to the Papal Academy for sciences Pope John Paul II stated that the Catholic Faith is not against the evolution theory as formulated by Charles Darwin."

May I just quote Darwin for a moment?
In the first place his revolutionary book was not called simply *The Origin of Species* as everyone thinks.

145

The exact title was *The Origin of Species by Natural Selection*, subtitled *The Preservation of Favoured Races in the Struggle for Life*.

Darwin wrote in a later book, *The Descent of Man*, "At some future period, not very distant as measured by centuries, the civilised races of man will almost certainly exterminate and replace the savage races throughout the world. At the same time the anthropomorphous apes . . . will no doubt be exterminated; the break between man and his nearest allies will be wider, for it will intervene between man in a more civilised state, as we may hope, even than the Caucasian, and some ape as low as a baboon, instead of now between the negro or Australian and the gorilla."*

From this belief sprouted the Holocaust, as Hitler was a devout Darwinist.

I hope someone will point out to the Pope what kind of teaching he is now supporting. He held out for a long time, by the way, many Protestant Churches having gone over to the side of the evolutionists a long time ago.

To summarise, the roman soldiers casting lots for Jesus' tunic could have been performing a prophetic task, without being aware of it.

They could have indicated a development in Christian history where the living "ecclesia" of the first centuries of our era changed into a great but dead body, an institution with power, money and worldly pomp. Scripture was completely externalised and became the letter without the spirit.

Only if the institutionalised Church had become the dead body of Christ can the history of Christianity be explained. In that case the crusades, the Inquisition and the silence about the Holocaust are not regrettable deviations from the truth, but proof that the Church as we know it *is* the world.

I say this with great sorrow, but I have no choice. If the official church (I am not talking about denominations, but about the Vatican, the World Council of Churches, the big bosses of Christianity and their organisations) were the body of Christ in the Pauline sense, then I would have to believe that Christ Himself inspired all the horrors of the Christian era. That cannot be.

Has then the Christian Church as we know it been a total failure, a tragic error?

* I found this quotation from Darwin in Henry Morris, *The Long War Against God*, p. 60.

No, the real miracle has been that on the whole the Christian Church has had a beneficial and civilising influence. Even though in my view it has come to represent the dead body of Christ, there was so much power left in that dead body, that the good far outweighed the evil. Moreover the Church was the guardian of the New Testament manuscripts, as the Jews were the guardians of the Old Testament.

An even greater miracle is that from time to time within the framework of the official churches in all denominations real saints have burst upon the scene. All through the ages men and women filled with the Holy Spirit, well known and also completely unknown, have been among us. My old minister van Dijk could be called a saintly man. And also outside the framework of the Church they could be found.

There is a beautiful story about a bishop who was travelling around the world, converting people right, left and centre. One day his ship put in at an island where he found three old men who lived there alone. They had never heard about Christianity, so the bishop decided to start with teaching them the Lord's Prayer. It took him a lot of trouble, because the three old men kept forgetting the words, but at last they managed it and, satisfied, the bishop left for his ship. The three old men took leave of him with deep, humble bows.

That night the ship stayed anchored one mile off the coast. Suddenly in the middle of the night the watchman cried out a warning. Everyone went on deck and the crew began to shiver with superstitious fright. There, over the water, plainly visible in the bright moonlight, walked the three old men. At last they reached the ship and seeing the bishop they apologized profusely for having disturbed his esteemed sleep but they were so worried that the ship might leave without them having noticed it. They would never then become holy because they had forgotten what came after "and lead us not into temptation".

I once more want to emphasize that I am not talking about specific churches. The underground church in the Soviet Empire during Stalin's rule of terror certainly was a living church with many martyrs. Richard Wurmbrand has described this period at length.

I also have the impression that the old living Christianity is often found in youth groups like Youth with a Mission and Youth for Christ. The work a man like Floyd McClung did in Amsterdam was beyond all praise.

In the healing ministries also one can often find the living body of Christ. I personally have seen real miracles happen there which means that the Holy Spirit is present in those communities.

So do not misunderstand me. I am not talking about living

churches in the sense of those churches that existed in the first centuries after Christ. They still exist. When I am talking about the Church as the dead body of Christ, what I rather have in mind are large bureaucratic institutions, which seem to specialise in power-politics. Let me give an example of what I mean.

I had a very gentle and also bright nun in my practice. For years on end she had been working among the sick in Central Africa. In the sixties a revolution took place and nearly all the nuns in her order were brutally raped.

When the troubles were over, one of the high officials of the World Council of Churches paid a visit to that country, if memory serves me right, as a guest of the new government. He also had a talk with the nuns who told him about their ordeal. In front of my patient he shrugged it off with the words, "You really have only yourselves to blame."

In his official position he could not say anything about cruelty committed in the name of the revolution.

That is what I mean by the "dead body of Christ". I believe that when David wrote Psalm 22 and looked into the far distant future, he foresaw the death of an official church that in his time had not even come into being.

Knowing what we do by now about making use of coincidence we must conclude that the development of the Christian Church as representative of Christ's dead body was not a haphazard error but fated to happen that way. When the goral is cast, God is not far away. He must have foreseen that the living church would get choked up in a political power game and would get entangled in the world, change into the world, stir up wars, help Nazi criminals to escape, bless weapons of destruction, profit from wars, and become unbelievably wealthy, while its Founder had not a place to lay His head.

He knew that those who pretended to represent Him would completely forget that He himself had expressly stated, just before He was murdered, that His kingdom was not of this world.

The small event of the four soldiers casting lots for Christ's tunic hides the terrible tragedy of a Church which became all powerful in a worldly sense and lost the only thing worth having, the Holy Spirit.

The story of the four soldiers is an impressive negative image of the real body of Christ, the one Paul speaks about in Ephesians 1:23.

Where then can we find the real body of Christ? It is still amongst us? For this we have to turn to the Last Supper.

I quote from Matthew 26:26: "And as they were eating, Jesus took bread and blessed it, brake it and gave it to the disciples and said: 'Take, eat, this is my body'."

Bullinger (in the Companion Bible Appendix 159) has pointed out the fact that the word "this" (this is my body) in the original Greek is neuter, and cannot agree with the word "bread" ("artos") because artos is masculine. *This* must then refer to the whole of the action: blessing . . . breaking . . . giving . . . eating.

The bread itself is not literally His body, it represents it in a metaphorical way and is used to bring home the truth that the *whole action* is His "body".

The emphasis lies, not on the substance, but on the doing, and this is one of the characteristics of both the Old and the New Testaments: it is always the doing that counts.

One of the best examples of this principle we find in Exodus 24:7 when Moses takes the Book of the Covenant (the commandments having just been given on Sinai) and reads it to the people. The people then answer, "All that the Lord hath spoken we will do and obey."

It is a pity that in the translation the real meaning of the verse is lost.

For "do and obey" we must read "do and hear", for that is what it says. Because it made no sense to the Bible translators in the 17th century it became "and obey".

"To hear" can also mean "to understand".

Now it becomes clearer. Only by doing what the Lord has commanded could one begin to understand. The doing came first, then the understanding.

Coming back to the Last Supper, the real body of Christ is not a visible religious organisation called a Church, but it consists of those who not only believe what the Lord has said (faith), but have also made it their own, acted upon it.

The priest in the concentration camp who took the place of a young man in the death bunker where prisoners were left in the dark without food and drink until they died, exemplified this attitude. Of course it is an extreme one, and it is to be hoped that most of will not be asked to go through such an ordeal, but those who belong to Christ's living body can be recognised by one main feature – charity (love). Without charity faith is dead.

A person full of faith but without charity may be very important in the organisation of the Church but such a person is not part of the body of Christ in the Pauline sense.

By the way it is the same grammatically, with the wine in the Last Supper as with the bread. Wine is masculine but the "This" in "this is My blood" is neuter. *This* cannot be applied to the wine as substance.

We are talking, however, about the body, so we will not go into the matter here.

Let me hasten to assure the reader that I do not belong to a sect which sees itself as the one and only body of Christ. According to my own definition I am not even a Christian, belonging to the body of Christ, as I score high on faith but extremely low on on charity indeed.

The body of Christ consists of those Christians, spread out through space and time, who believed in Him *and acted upon His word*, practising charity.

They were sometimes members of a church, sometimes not. If an organised church is lucky, there are members of the body of Christ in its midst. The chance of finding them outside the organised church is probably as great as finding them within. In short, what we call a Church and what Paul calls the body of Christ are two completely different conceptions.

In this New Testament example we have met another aspect of coincidence – fate stepping in and directing the course of history. Prophecy and coincidence are united in a single event.

Slowly but surely the answer to the great question "WHAT IS COINCIDENCE?" draws nearer.

Before ending this chapter we must ask: "Should we reintroduce the casting of lots? Should we consult the *I Ching*, the Tarot, Astrology? Do they have a place in modern life? As everyone knows who visits bookshops there is an enormous upsurge of interest in these subjects.

As I said before I personally don't believe that we should turn to them. They have become very much outmoded. They are interesting relics of the past, such as the notion of flat earth, but we are moving into a completely new era – that of the Holy Spirit – where God answers questions in a direct way.

People often say to me, "God does not answer my prayers. I have given up praying."

I then advise them to write down their request in a diary. Often their prayers are fulfilled in such a quiet and gentle way that they do not even notice and only afterwards realise that their request has been granted.

Whatever happened to the goral that was once so important in the whole of the ancient world? Has the casting of lots become completely obsolete?

No, the habit is still very much with us, only the name has been changed. We do not call it casting lots any more, but casting votes. The goral has become the ballot box, but as we don't believe any more it is very much to be doubted if the result is God's will.

FUN AND DRAMA go together like fleas and a dog. Many a joke was born in a tight corner. I have suggested already that the Creator loves fun. He has a great sense of humour. This aspect of Him is seldom mentioned and I do not understand why. His Son was born to one of the wittiest peoples in the world.

Beside an American highway there was a huge poster announcing, "JESUS IS THE ANSWER". Someone had written under it, "But what was the question?"

Jesus could have written it Himself. We never read in the Bible that He laughed, but He must have done so.

I realise of course that there is an awe-inspiring aspect to God. One only has to look at the starry heavens to realise this and when Proverbs 1:7 says, "The fear of the Lord is the beginning of knowledge", it is this aspect which is meant. "Fear" is not "being afraid of", but "being in awe of". The Hebrew word for fear has as its root the verb "to see". When I see His works I am overwhelmed by their greatness.

On the other hand I am convinced of His sense of humour. Genesis 1:27 says that God created man in his own image. One of the most striking traits of the human race, even in terrible circumstances, is a sense of humour and a propensity for telling jokes and laughing. Yesterday I had a three-year-old slightly retarded boy in my office. His mother told me that he had difficulty in understanding her words, but all the time with a wide smile he was poking fun at me.

Laughter and children go together. If we, as human beings, are made in God's image and if we, as human beings, are the only entities here on earth who can laugh and crack jokes, surely this wit comes from Him?

I sometimes wonder if all the solemnity hasn't made people a bit suspicious of heaven. I once saw a cartoon where a man in a long white garment with wings on his back and a harp in his hand sat on a cloud. The face of the man was that of an elderly shopkeeper whose love of fun was evident in his face. Yet, just at that moment he was a bit bewildered (amazing how a good draughtsman can show all these things in a little drawing). An angel comes along and the man with the wings asks him, "Say, you don't mean that this goes on forever?"

At the end of Goethe's *Faust* – if memory serves me right – the angels say to Faust, "Wer immer strebend sich bemüht, den können wir erlösen" ("He who is always preoccupied with working very hard to get on can be saved by us").

I don't believe a word of it. One of our evangelists, Anne van der Bijl, once said to me, "Do you know why the priests in the Old

Testament wore linen garments? Because what they had to do was not heavy and sweaty but joyful and light."

The principle is demonstrated in the following conversation between a Roman Catholic priest and a Rabbi:–

"I don't understand your priesthood. You are a rabbi and you stay a rabbi. No possibility of promotion," said the priest.

"What do you mean?" the rabbi asked.

"Well, I am a simple priest, but I might be a bishop one day."

"So what?" retorted the rabbi.

"As a matter of fact," the priest continued, "it's not totally impossible that one day I'll make cardinal."

"Is that a fact?" said the rabbi, unimpressed.

"I might even become the Pope!" the priest exclaimed, carried away by his own eloquence.

"So what?" the rabbi said again.

Now the priest got very irritated and exclaimed, "Well, what else do you want me to become? God?"

The rabbi looked up with a deprecating smile and said, "One of our boys did just that, you know."

Considering these things, it is not to be wondered at that the creative background of our existence, which peeps around the corner in coincidences, makes us laugh. Good coincidences often have their humorous side.

When we analyse the essence of jokes they are in principle coincidences. The seemingly haphazard "falling together" of two unrelated facts or meanings tickles our laughing muscles.

There is nothing more deadly to a joke than to explain it, but let me give some examples and let the reader spot the *double entendre*.

First, courtesy of Mrs von Pein who sent them to me from the USA, some English signs in foreign countries:–

In a Japanese hotel: "You are invited to take advantage of the chambermaid".

In a Zürich hotel: "Because of the impropriety of entertaining guests of the opposite sex in the bedroom, we suggest that you use the lobby for that purpose".

In a Norwegian cocktail bar: "Ladies are requested not to have children in the bar".

And still by courtesy of Mrs von Pein:–

At a Bible school: " Syntax is all the money collected in church from sinners".

"The people who followed the Lord were called the 12 opossums".

Laughter nowadays is seen as playing a part in cancer therapy. The editor of the Wessex Cancer Help Centre Newsletter, besides always publishing knowledgeable articles, sees to it that we can relax: "Dear milkman. Just had a baby. Please leave another one."

Or, from a church magazine: "Don't let worry kill you. Let the Church help."

And from an insurance claim: "The pedestrian had no idea which way to run, so I ran over him."

I hope you're starting to realise that these things are funny because two unconnected factors rub up against each other and kindle a spark. Jokes are coincidences with a bushy tail.

Mr Cohen has a severe phobia. He cannot sleep at night as he knows that a tiger is lurking under his bed. As soon as he falls asleep the tiger will crawl out from under the bed and eat him.

He doesn't sleep a wink and neither tranquillizers nor other pills from his doctor help him. He is referred to a psychiatrist who starts a psychoanalysis. After a year he knows nearly everything about his youth but he still does not sleep a wink, because he is absolutely sure the tiger is there under his bed. Suddenly he stops going to the psychiatrist. The good doctor worries about Mr Cohen (and about his lucrative client) and rings him up.

"I am healed," says Mr Cohen.

"What? All of a sudden?"

"No, I went to the rabbi."

"Whatever did he do?"

"He didn't do anything. When I told him there was a tiger under my bed he told me to saw the legs off my bed."

In this case it is a little bit more difficult to see the coming together of two independent factors. Yet it is there, only hidden, just like the tiger.

A joke from that Amsterdam king of Jewish joke tellers, Max Tailleur:—

"Samuel is on a journey and stays in a hotel. He finds a Bible and, rather bored, he begins to rifle through the pages.

On the first page he finds, 'If you are ill, read Psalm 103, if you are anxious about your family, read Psalm 34, if you are lonely, read Psalm 23.'

He turns to Psalm 23 and sees at the bottom of the page a message, written with a ballpoint pen.

'If you are as lonely as before, ring room no. 42 and ask for Nelly'."

And then of course there is the little snake asking his mother, "Mum, are we the sort of snakes that strangle our prey, or do we kill it with poison?"

"Why do you want to know?" his mother asks.

"I've just bitten my lip."

It is not easy to pinpoint why we laugh. We are for a moment tuned in to that great ocean of joy, bubbling beneath the surface of our lives, where laughing comes naturally and understanding quicker than comprehension.

Now that you have been properly inoculated against thunder and lightning, let us proceed with drama.

What better beginning than Shakespeare's *King Lear*, Act III, Scene 1:–

"Kent: 'I know you, where is the King?'

Gentleman: 'Contending with the fretful elements;
           Bids the wind blow the earth into the sea,
           Or swell the curled waters 'bove the main,
           that things might change or cease; tears his white hair,
           which the impetus blasts, with eyeless rage,
           catch in their fury, and make nothing of;
           Strive in his little world of man to out-scorn
           and to-and-fro conflicting wind and rain.'"

On 3 May 1987 an English friend called Leon and his wife Sally were staying in my house. They had the guest room on the second floor looking west over the city and towards the distant dunes. From my house it is about 4 miles to the North Sea as the crow flies.

During the evening we were in the sitting-room on the ground floor, also facing west.

It appeared that Leon was something of an expert on Shakespeare, though he is a dentist by profession.

He started to tell me a lot about the background to some of the plays by the great poet. At one moment he began to tell me about *King Lear*.

As English readers know, one of the most dramatic scenes takes place during a violent storm.

While we were still deep in *King Lear*, one of those sudden westerly storms struck the coastal region.

Leon, as a good Englishman, had left the bedroom window wide open and the storm tore the whole window out, frame and all, and tossed it onto the slanting roof with a shattering noise.

Then it sailed down and crashed just behind our sitting room outside on the flagstones. It was a spectacular accompaniment to the story of the mad old king.

For the next story I have to explain my standpoint on Darwin's theory of evolution.

There exist two irreconcilable schools of thought about the origin of our world. They are called the evolutionists and the creationists. The evolutionists think that this world evolved just by itself, the creationists think that the world was created by God. There is an in-between school which teaches that God created the world with the help of evolution. That is like having your cake and eating it.

Up until the French Revolution, 200 years ago, all major scientists were what we now call "creationists". They believed that in the beginning God created the heavens and the earth. They also believed that because an intelligent Creator had made this world, laws could be discovered in an orderly manner. One could say that thanks to their faith, sciences, as we now understand it, became possible.

They followed the advice of Proverbs 1:7, which I have mentioned before.

Henry Morris in his book *Men of Science, Men of God* lists 108 of the most important scientists who believed in the creation exactly as described in Genesis 1.

Among them were Leonardo da Vinci, Johan Keppler, Francis Bacon, Blaise Pascal, Robert Boyle, Galileo, Copernicus, William Harvey, Isaac Newton, Linnaeus, Faraday, Morse, Bell, Dalton, Prout, Pasteur, Mendel, all household-names for anyone with a high school education.

After the French Revolution, and certainly after Darwin, the paradigm of science shifted towards evolution as the explanation for the origin of our world.

Evolution is nowadays the leading religion. I call it a religion on purpose as there exists no actual evidence for the validity of the evolution theory. As one scientist recently (1997) said, "It needs an awful lot of faith to keep believing in it."

On the other hand several scientists who are not directly connected with the Bible have, after careful research, come to the conclusion that our world must have been made by design (Denton, Behe).

Darwin predicted the finding of many so-called "missing links" between the different species, but after digging for 135 years the evolutionists have not found one single missing link. Though within one species there is a lot of variety going on, the species themselves strictly keep to their bounds. Calling this variety within species "evolution", as is done, confuses the issue. "Limited adaptation" or "playful variation" would be better descriptions.

The lack of proof for Darwin's theory led to the preposterous

155

prank of a museum director (helped by the great evolution guru, Teilhard de Chardin it is whispered), who constructed a missing link between a human being and an ape, using a human skull and the under-jaw of an ape, which became known as the Piltdown Man. For decades it proudly figured as one of the proofs in favour of evolution.

Today they call the Piltdown Man a hoax, now that the swindle has been discovered, but I myself think that the evolutionists had begun to grow desperate and badly needed a stimulant.

Seeing that digging up fossils would deny them the missing links they so urgently needed, the "Neo-Darwinists" came up with an even more weird hypothesis, one of the most ridiculous ever invented – the hopeful monster theory by Goldschmidt.

According to this theory a reptile produced an egg one day and out crept a complete bird. The chance of a huge amount of spontaneous genetic mutations necessary for such a jump all happening at the same time is so small that it can only be described as a statistical impossibility.

According to Denton in his book *Evolution, a Theory in Crisis* it is equivalent to believing in miracles.

It is only in the second half of the 20th century that scientists – devoutly believing in evolution – have taken evolution into their own hands and are now mixing genes of different species. Mixing human genes with those of a pig (probably to make better dictators) yielded a hog with gout, but far more dangerous is the genetic manipulation of our food.

When man thinks he can improve on creation, he usually ends up with a catastrophe.

Take for instance genetically-altered soya. What exactly has been done to this food?

In the first place, why was it done at all?

They said it was necessary to make it possible for soya plants to survive being sprayed with strong herbicides.

A far stronger argument, though, seems to be that one cannot license plants growing naturally, but if one alters a plant genetically one can take out a licence on it and straightaway one has a monopoly.

Two new genes were built into the genetic material of soya:–

1. Genes from Agrobacterium Tumefaciens. The "tumour-making bacteria" this means. It causes cancer in plants. After this new gene had been implanted, the soya bean contained a new enzyme which had never before been part of the human diet. The long-term effects are unknown.

2. Genes from the cauliflower mosaic virus. It is related to the virus

responsible for the dangerous Hepatitis B infection and also the virus one finds in AIDS patients (there is still a lot of fighting going on over the question as to whether it causes AIDS or not, but it seems to me an unsociable guest). Dr Joseph Cummins, a retired professor of genetics, thinks this is the most dangerous of the two.

In 1997 15% of American soya production will be derived from genetically-altered plants, which could be biological time-bombs.

If this were all, we could simply stop eating soya, but there is far more to it than meets the eye.

Soya is also used as raw material for soy-lecithin and soya oil. Soy-lecithin is used in a host of foods and one cannot find out if it is derived from genetically-altered soya.

It only says on the packet "lecithin", or "E 322". To avoid it is extremely difficult.

As I said earlier, scientists do not know the long-term effects and simply hope for the best. It is the same thing as with the atom bomb. When they exploded the first one in the Nevada desert, they simply hoped that the chain-reaction would stop by itself, but they were not quite sure at the time. There was a chance that it might have gone on and in that case I would not be typing this book now, neither would you be reading it.

In this gene manipulation business they play a game of wait-and-see, but it is a game with our health at stake, let us make no mistake about it. The scientists can do this with a clear conscience, because their basic belief is not in creation but evolution. They play the role of God, have taken evolution (as they think) into their own hands and if, inadvertently, a catastrophe befalls us, it will be a question of the survival of the fittest, completely in accordance with evolutionary teaching.

The theory of evolution always reminds me of that well-known female scientist in Lewis Carroll's *Through the Looking Glass*, the White Queen.

Alice says somewhere, "There's no use trying . . . one *can't* believe impossible things" and the White Queen, urging her to believe the impossible says, "When I was your age, I always did it for half-an-hour a day. Why, sometimes I've believed as many as six impossible things before breakfast."

From the superb book *The Red King's Dream* by Jo Elwyn Jones and J. Francis Gladstone I learned that Carroll was a determined opponent of Darwin. It was during the period when Carroll was writing his Alice books that Darwin began to throw his weight about.

The two writers think that in the story of the Duchess' baby changing into a pig (*Alice in Wonderland*) Carroll actually might have been pulling Darwin's leg by making evolution go backwards.

This explanation was necessary for the following story:–

One of my patients was friendly with a female professor at a university in the USA. She had brought this friend to my home a couple of times and we had found that we had much in common, as we both called ourselves Christians and liked to discuss the Bible. My relationship with this lady was quite friendly.

On 4 July 1994 the two women came to visit again. It had been a warm morning and the weather was sultry. I was upstairs in my study when at 11 a.m. the bell rang and I heard my wife opening the front door.

At the very moment that the good professor crossed our threshold, there was a violent flash of lightning and simultaneously an ear-splitting thunderclap which shook the whole house. It was the beginning of a heavy thunderstorm which lasted for two hours.

While we were drinking a cup of coffee the professor told me about her university. Suddenly she said, "I am very indignant about what has happened recently. In one of our departments the new professor has been appointed and he turns out to be a creationist!"

I told the good Professor that I myself was a creationist and proceeded to give her my arguments, just as I have explained them above.

The result was staggering. She simply exploded. The whole room seemed electrically charged, she was livid with rage.

She broke off her visit as soon as she could without being impolite and vanished with my patient in her car into the thunderstorm. Later my patient told me that the whole journey back home, while the car crawled slowly through the heavy rain, she had been foaming at the mouth, storming against my insolence in doubting beliefs held by the whole scientific community. It was only a couple of hours later that the coincidence struck me: the totally unexpected thunderbolt when she crossed the threshold and the completely unlooked-for explosion when I explained my standpoint on evolution.

I never heard from her again.

Earlier in this book I mentioned the cluster of coincidences in November 1996 when our group was monitoring them.

On 19 November one of my patients told me the following story.

One of her best friends had a teenage daughter who, with another girl and two boys, had gone by car to a conference in Germany. They had started very early in the morning and were driving through Germany during the first hour of dawn.

They were talking and the conversation turned towards death. One of the girls said, "Well, if one has to die, it seems better to me that it should happen at a single stroke".

The rest agreed with her and at that moment the driver suddenly saw looking up before him in the dim morning light a parked truck. With all his strength he tugged at the wheel and the car swerved aside, began to skid and hit the truck sideways. Then the car came to a stop.

"Wow!" he said. "That was a near miss!"

He looked at his three companions and they were all dead.

It was he who related the conversation that had taken place just prior to the catastrophe.

Premonition? Coincidence? It is extremely difficult to draw conclusions from a terrible event like that, but I do not think it was just a chance conversation.

In June 1993 I was on holiday in Spain and I wrote the second book for Mara. Actually in the sequence it was the last, taking place in our time. It portrayed the life of a girl called Lilianne, who lived in the Netherlands and had been born in 1980.

Though she is still very young she discovers a terrible secret. Scientists and Nazi-like occultists are conspiring to take control of the whole human race. All life on earth is threatened by this conspiracy and the powers protecting humanity allow Lilianne to go back in time four years as, by altering some seemingly small events, she can thwart the criminal plans of the conspirators. For reasons I cannot further explain here she is the only one who can change the fate of humanity.

I must now try to summarise pages 91–103 of the book *Lilianne* which is necessary in order to understand the extremely strange cluster of coincidences connected with those pages.

In the course of her adventures Lilianne has managed to hide herself in a hotel where the élite of the secret society is holding a meeting and she is able to eavesdrop on the whole of the proceedings.

Here is what she discovers.

One of the main speakers is a Dutch professor called Dirk Slager. This man gives an exposition of the aims of the secret society and the means by which it is going to attain them.

The central aim is to create a humanity devoid of free will, governed by a small élite.

He shows slides of the human brain and tells his audience that in

Nazi Germany the "control button" of free will in the brain has been located. Human beings whose control button has been switched off look like normal people but in reality they are zombies, totally obedient to their rulers.

What now follows is real history, though written in fictional form for Mara.

In 1938 the discovery was made that fluoride could reduce the capacity for free will. It was not a spectacular decrease but nevertheless it could be measured. That was why Hitler wanted to fluoridate the water supply in occupied countries – to keep resistance to a minimum.

After the war fluoridation of the water supply started in the USA, purportedly, to prevent tooth decay (and here fiction takes over again) but in reality – the professor assured his audience – to assert greater control over people's minds.

He went on to tell his audience that a special organisation within the élite, called "Delta-sigma-delta" (the name is borrowed from the real world) had specialised in such chemical control of humanity.

Since the effect of fluoride on free will had been discovered, scientists had tried their utmost to convince politicians to fluoridate the water supply of the largest possible part of humanity, expecting that eventually a substance would be found that worked even more effectively than fluoride.

If such a compound could be discovered the only thing one had to do was switch from fluoride to this new stuff. As the fluoridation equipment was already in place this would be a simple operation.

At this point Professor Dirk Slager paused dramatically and proceeded to announce that the new substance had actually been manufactured. The numbing effect of fluoride on the exercise of free will had been enhanced a thousandfold by binding the mineral to a protein derived from the extremely dangerous Black Widow spider.

People drinking only very small amounts of this substance for one month once and for all lost their free will.

Dirk Slager showed a new slide. Again one saw the human brain but in the part where the capacity for free will was located could now be seen a distinct blot of calcium.

"Tests on criminals have shown," he said, "that the bit of the brain which controls free will has been destroyed and changed into a calcified scar.

As many countries are not yet fluoridated – more's the pity – another way of distributing the poison has been developed. The effect takes slightly longer to achieve complete success but in the long run it is the same as the one caused by poisoning the water.

We can put the new substance in toothpaste, enabling it to penetrate the mucous layer of the mouth and eventually reach the brain.

During the year that we are depriving humanity of its free will, the élite should of course, abstain rather from the doctored water or the new toothpaste." (Laughter)

"The new compound will be praised as the ultimate prevention of tooth decay and be called 'carioclast'."

There was now a short pause in the meeting and then Professor Dirk Slager explained the second major aim of the élite.

"A special committee of our inner circle has discovered the real difficulty on earth. It has carefully studied history in all its aspects, especially that of the last 250 years, and come to the conclusion that the enormous proliferation of human life, the population explosion, is the cause of all evils."

"We have," he said proudly, "at last found an ideal method to curb this teeming fertility and bring the world population back to acceptable proportions."

The professor then proceeded to talk about the ozone layer that protects humanity against the devastating effects of solar radiation.

The layer is, as we all know, already deteriorating under the influence of several man-made factors, one of them being space missiles.

"But now," Dirk Slager said, "we will destroy the ozone layer on purpose in order to cull humanity and other proliferating life to 1% of its present numbers."

(In this part of the story I was definitely influenced by a similar plan developed by the mad Professor Filostrato in *That Hideous Strength* by C. S. Lewis.)

"As long as the elimination process lasts," said Dirk Slager, "the élite and their passive and totally obedient slaves will be living under enormous protective domes."

His next slides depicted a map of the world on which were drawn factories with high chimneys, located at the North and South Poles. From those chimneys little arrows spiralled away around the earth towards the equator.

"There," he said, "are the ozone-layer-destroying factories. Until its free will has been eliminated, the public will be told that they are engaged in restoring the ozone layer, but in reality they are spewing out huge amounts of chlorofluorocarbons (CFCs), among the most powerful destroyers of ozone we know." (This again is scientific fact,

CFCs being indeed instrumental in destroying the ozone layer. They come from refrigerators and spraycans.)

At this point a woman in the audience asked if it was pure chance that a fluoride compound should be used both to destroy free will and the ozone layer.

"A good question," said Dirk Slager.

At this point reality takes over from fiction again. The following thesis is one I developed at a great dentists' congress in Belgium.

"There are three sorts of elements on this earth.

The first enhance and maintain life. They are called 'essential' as without them we cannot live. Here is a short list: calcium, magnesium, oxygen, hydrogen, nitrogen, phosphorous, carbon, iron.

There are also essential trace elements like zinc, manganese, silica, copper, chromium, cobalt, etc. Only tiny amounts of them are necessary, but without them we would die. We need a mere one-millionth of a gram of cobalt every day, but if we do not get it, we cannot make red blood cells.

Then there are the neutral elements, like helium, argon, etc. They have no known physiological function in our bodies.

Finally there are those elements that are detrimental to life. They shorten our lives and they are also in a certain sense essential – not for the individual but for humanity as a whole. They see to it that we age and die, and that one generation makes room for the next one. Arsenic is one of them. The most active, however, is fluoride. That is why – as we get older – the fluoride content in our bodies slowly increases."

"That is why we use this element for both the ozone layer and the free will as it is an element of destruction." (This last sentence is from the fictional world of the book.)

This is all we need to know to grasp the significance of the following coincidences. Let me summarise:–

1. In 1993 I wrote this book and from 1 September 1993 onward for exactly one year it was read to Mara.

2. The group of criminal scientists sought total control over the minds of the human population.

3. They used in pursuit of this goal an enhanced form of the mineral, fluoride.

4. Factories were built at the North and South Poles to attack the ozone layer.

5. The world population will be reduced by these special factories pouring CFCs into the ozone layer.

6. Slides with little arrows showed the distribution of the gas in the upper layers of the atmosphere.

7. The exact time the conspiracy was planning to take over the world was the last decade of the 20th century.

Now for the coincidences.

In September 1996 I opened my German medical journal *Raum & Zeit*. On page 5 I found a leading article about an ultra-secret military project cooked up by the military-industrial complex of the USA.

In 1994 at a lonely spot in Alaska a gigantic field of aerials had been built. Certain independent researchers got the wind up and discovered that there were plans to beam up unbelievably strong electromagnetic waves towards the ionised layer surrounding the earth. This layer is intimately bound up with the ozone layer. The reason for bringing this layer "to the boil" was not quite clear to me but the nickname of the project, "Skybuster", sounded ominous. The official name of this project was HAARP (High Frequency Active Auroral Research Project), a totally misleading name as research played only a minor part. When I saw the picture of this extensive field of aerials I was straightaway reminded of the lecture given by Professor Dirk Slager in the book *Lilianne*, in which he had unfolded his sinister plans.

Then I forgot all about it until in the spring of 1997 someone wrote to me, suggesting I read a book written about the HAARP project. It was available in the American Book Center in Amsterdam. It was called *Angels Don't Play This HAARP* and was written by Jeanne Manning and Dr Nick Begich.

There was that HAARP again. I asked for the book for my birthday.

On 7 June 1997 I started this book about coincidences. I had not planned to include the similarity between the HAARP and *Lilianne* because I thought it was too weak. Then at the beginning of July I began to read the HAARP book and immediately understood that including the story had become a must.

What sort of a crazy idea is this to bring the ionic layer to the boil? The military authorities knew from extensive research on a smaller scale, and also from similar projects in the former Soviet Union (the Woodpecker Transmissions), that manipulating the stratosphere could interrupt radio communications, change the weather and do other amusing things. There is a considerable possibility that the HAARP project can also hurt eco-systems, harm human physiology, and disrupt both mental and corporal functions.

Let no one think that responsible authorities would never do such an outrageous thing.

Do not put your trust in governments.

In our century everything that can be done seems to be allowable for the single reason that it is technically possible. In a time without intrinsic morals one cannot expect protection against immoral behaviour by the government. What is the government anyhow? Just an expression of the paradigm of our age. What is the central paradigm today? That everything is relative. Absolute values do not exist any more. Everything goes as long as it is called SCIENCE, the new idol of our time.

AS CHANCE
WOULD HAVE IT

On page 88 of the book *Angels Don't Play This Haarp* Elisabeth Rauscher is mentioned as someone who, as long ago as 1984, warned that recent technology could produce weapon-systems with which all life on earth could be more efficiently wiped out.

The scientists involved in HAARP do not quite know what will happen when HAARP is fully operational and realises its full potential. An unstoppable chain-reaction is not unthinkable, which would bring devastating destruction to the whole earth. This uncertainty – similar to that which surrounded the first atom bomb – will not stop the scientists. They take a risk with us and our descendants, but why not? Let the fittest survive. . . .

But there is more about HAARP, and it was this aspect especially which decided me to include the story.

On those unbelievably powerful electromagnetic beams a second wavelength can be made to ride piggyback, so to speak, and this second wavelength is in the range of 10–20 Hertz or even lower. It is called "ELF", which stands for "Extreme Low Frequency". This is the range of frequencies the human brain uses for its activities.

The technique exists already which, with the help of these ELF waves – can completely change human thinking and human emotions. This can work not only on people standing in front of the radiation machine but at a distance of hundreds of miles. The ELF waves riding with the powerful waves bounce off the stratosphere enabling them to change human behaviour in whole regions.

Literally speaking it is now possible to manipulate the human will and it can be done invisibly and at a distance.

When I read this well-documented story I was reminded of my assistant days in a psychiatric hospital. There were always patients suffering from schizophrenia, who thought that they were being influenced against their will by invisible radiation. I even remember one patient in Leyden who told us that just outside the city there were large electrical works supplying him with the electric current he ran on. Now and then, he said, they would cut off the current, and he would be totally paralysed whenever that happened.

Indeed, from time to time, he would suddenly stop in the middle of doing something and fall into a catatonic trance which could last from a couple of minutes to a couple of hours. When he recovered he was always extremely angry at the people in the works who had done it again.

Strangely enough, apart from this delusion, he was completely normal and went about his work as a repairer of bicycles in the hospital in a cheerful way.

I now ask myself if these patients were a species of prophets, foreseeing what was brewing in a not too distant future. Out of the mouths of babes and drunkards comes the truth. Must a certain group of psychotic patients be added to those two?

Now comes the part of the book *Angels Don"t Play This HAARP* that really blew my mind.

The military application of all these discoveries about ELF waves can be made even more effective by introducing minute amounts of certain minerals into the water supplies of those regions where one wants to influence the population. The water supplies are not the only possible vehicle. One has other options for the distribution.

As soon as these minerals have entered the bodies of the victims one can enhance their potency enormously by transmitting the right frequencies. Take, for instance, lithium, which is mentioned in the book. It is well known that lithium has a strong influence on the emotions and can be used in the treatment of certain psychotic illnesses. By giving a minute amount of lithium to the patient and then beaming the right frequency at him, one can change the inactive small amount into a very active substance.

Fluoride is not mentioned in the book, but we know that fluoride has a dulling effect on mental faculties. Chinese scientists confirmed this in 1996 from comparative studies and in the USA animal tests (with rats) have also proven the stupid-making effect of fluoride. One could imagine a fluoridated population being mentally dulled in an extremely powerful way, when the right frequency was beamed at it, thus enhancing the feeble workings of fluoride on the mind a thousandfold.

If this conception is right it is a sobering thought that 50% of the USA and 10% of the UK are fluoridated.

What this amounts to is that minerals in quantities far below the toxic dosage could become highly active when bombarded by the right frequencies, thus affecting all those human beings who have been ingesting minute doses of those minerals in their purified form.

The scientists concocting these horrors have stated – as the documents conform – that the élite would have to abstain from those minerals.

It also becomes clear from the book that these atrocities are not aimed at a foreign enemy exclusively. It is quite openly said that these new techniques can also be used against "adversaries of the Government".

Everything I have just written is so important that I will refer to something on page 167 in order to sum up: "Small amounts of chemicals in a person's physiological system in amounts below normal levels where negative physical effects are known to occur will have no perceivable effects *until* radiation on a radio frequency is introduced."

On page 205 one can see a drawing with little arrows going towards the stratosphere, emanating from the installation.

We can now compare *Lilianne* with *Angels Don't Play This HAARP* and demonstrate a whole cluster of coincidences.

1. HAARP was being built in 1994 during the time when *Lilianne* was being read to Mara.

2. A small scientific élite in *Lilianne* sought total control over the human population.

A group of scientists, seeing themselves as an élite, according to the HAARP book, has discovered a way of gaining control over people's minds any place on earth.

3. In *Lilianne* chemically-enhanced fluoride was introduced to the water supplies or toothpaste. The aim – dulling the mind and the free will.

In pursuit of this same goal the HAARP scientists put certain minerals into the water supplies or used other methods. They are enhanced not chemically but by electromagnetic radiation.

4. In *Lilianne* the installations necessary for emitting CFCs into the stratosphere were situated at the North and South Poles.

The HAARP installation for boiling the stratosphere is in Alaska.

5. In *Lilianne* the élite is warned to abstain from the chemically-enhanced fluoride in order not to become mentally dull.

The HAARP élite is warned not to drink or eat the minerals in order to avoid the devastating effect of the ELF waves.

6. In *Lilianne* the ozone layer is destroyed on purpose in order to cull the world's population. Other eco-systems also suffer from the destruction.

HAARP threatens eco-systems, in short, life on earth, by its deliberate boiling of the ionized and ozone layer. A runaway effect from the "Skybuster" is considered not to be impossible. One takes a calculated risk.

7. In *Lilianne* the exact time when the conspirators want to take over the world is the last decade of the 20th century.

The HAARP installation become operational in 1996.

In both cases the scientists are quite mad to take the risk, of course.

8. In *Lilianne* Dirk Slager shows a graph with little arrows pointing from the installations upwards to demonstrate the distribution of CFCs.

In the book about the HAARP there is a drawing of little arrows pointing upwards to show the path of the ELF waves.

9. Both in *Lilianne* and this book about the HAARP we have descriptions of how to dull the minds of the population.

In my view we have a clear case of a cluster of coincidences between the book *Lilianne* and the book *Angels Don't Play This HAARP*.

Let us just imagine that the book *Angels Don't Play This HAARP* is just a wash-out, a paranoia à deux of the two writers. Something they put together from scraps and made into a horror story.

Even then the coincidences are there, be it only between their book and mine.

I do not believe, however, that they are wrong. I believe they are dead right and that the coincidences between the two books are not restricted to the books alone: the real coincidences are between the book *Lilianne* and reality.

I only wanted to demonstrate that regardless of the angle one looks at it from, the clustering of at least 9 coincidences remains intact.

One more remark must be added.

Do not think, please, that I am some weird clairvoyant, seeing into the future. I am nothing of the sort, just a plain MD with his normal ration of common sense.

The only thing I wanted to highlight is the mystery of coincidence.

The next two coincidences happened during the Second World War and both saved my life.

By August 1944 the Allied armies had swept north and east through France and Belgium and were nearing the Dutch border. In our country something strange happened. It was 5 September 1944, a Tuesday, and suddenly rumours took hold of the whole population. The Allies had crossed the rivers . . . they had taken Rotterdam . . . they had taken the Hague. They were nearing Haarlem! People retrieved their orange bunting and their red-white-and-blue flags from hiding places and here and there they were standing along the roads leading south, eagerly awaiting the liberators. The Quislings (as the Dutch and Scandinavian traitors were called in England) were fleeing to the east, in the direction of Germany, because they also believed the rumours. We even saw German troops leaving our region.

The tension became nearly unbearable. "Mad Tuesday" that day has been called ever since and of course it was just a terrible illusion.

Then came 17 September and Operation Market Garden. On 19 September in that part of the municipality where I lived, those who were north of a certain line were given three days' notice to evacuate the area. Why this happened never became clear. They said an invasion of Ijmuiden was expected, but this was nonsense. Probably it was more to do with terrorising the population.

We all had to find temporary shelter at short notice, but the Germans made this extra difficult for us by confiscating every bicycle they saw.

Nevertheless my father rode his 6 miles south and every time a German soldier tried to steal it he cursed the man so soundly that he kept his means of transport. At last he arrived at the house of friends* in the same municipality. They lived south of the evacuation line and thus were allowed to stay. He told them about our predicament and they invited us to stay with them for the couple of days it would take the Allies to liberate us (we really talked like that in those days).

We left our house and went to stay with our friends and then came that devastating disappointment when the battle of Arnhem was lost. The Allies stayed south of the Rhine.

London had ordered a great railway strike in preparation for the liberation of our country and all trains stopped. The Germans were furious and all food transport stopped. Slowly but surely a long, cold winter approached without electricity, without gas and increasingly without food. It is still remembered as the "Famine Winter". Between 2000 and 3000 people died from lack of food. Some say the toll was greater.

For many young men of my age the streets had become very dangerous indeed. The Germans hunted all of us relentlessly for slave labour in their factories manufacturing what was necessary for the war. Many young men had gone underground, staying with farmers in the polders, where there was still enough food. It was easier to hide there than in the cities.

For an understanding of what follows one needs to know a little

---

* These were the parents of Gerrit, mentioned on page 86, who a year earlier had been thrown out of their country house to make place for the Germans.

about Haarlem. The city is surrounded by a ring of municipalities, the largest being Bloemendaal between Haarlem and the dunes bordering the sea.

Standing among the dunes, and quite near to where we were now living with our friends, was an enormous concrete anti-tank wall, separating us from the roads to the sea. The Germans hoped to withstand an attack from the coast with that wall.

On 5 December many boys came home during the day from their underground hideouts to celebrate the St Nicolas festival with their families. While they were sneaking home secretly, they were not aware of the fact that the Germans knew quite well what was going on and took their cue from the old nursery-rhyme: " 'Come into my parlour' said the spider to the fly".

During the night German troops silently drew an iron cordon around Haarlem and the surrounding villages, starting at the outer fringes of the suburbs. An hour before dawn they began a huge round-up. Slowly and methodically they worked inwards, house after house and street after street.

I happened to live just near the fringe where the great manhunt started and at 7 a.m. I was wakened by our host who said that I'd better get dressed as there was a lot of activity going on in the street. He left my room and I picked up a match to light the oil lamp. My small bedroom was situated near the front door and there was no curtain at the window.

Just as I was about to strike the match, an uneasy feeling crept over me and I looked at the window. There, rifle in hand, stood a German soldier, trying to peer into the dark room. I froze, slowly lowered myself to the floor and crawled towards the hall. Then I ran upstairs to warn my friend Gerrit, who had come home that night from his hiding-place in the polder. We both grabbed raincoats and he a pair of shoes and we ran to the back door which we cautiously opened. There was a lot of shouting going on in the streets, but here everything was quiet. There was no hiding-place in our house and we planned to get away from the round-up, having no idea of its extent. So, while a German soldier hammered on the front door, yelling for it to be opened, we slipped through the back door.

Our bare feet touched the covering of snow but we did not feel any cold. We crossed several gardens and two roads, making for the dunes. At last we reached the street that bordered the dunes. I had planned to cross part of the dunes, heading southeast towards the house of my friend's uncle, about 1½ miles away. Hopefully we would then have left the round-up behind us.

Just as we were about the cross the road I saw the dark shape of a German truck approaching. We threw ourselves into a ditch and I saw the truck full of heavily-armed soldiers silhouetted against the night sky. Happily, our dark raincoats hid the lighter colour of our pyjamas. Gerrit hastily put on his shoes and then we stole into the dunes. Pale moonlight illuminated our way and we began to run, I in front.

I still remember my mood. It was extremely alert, very much in the here and now, and even then it struck me that I wasn't making a beeline for the house we had in mind, but following a strange meandering trajectory, now circling a dune to the right, then round a cluster of trees to the left, on and on, as if an invisible force was steering me while I only obeyed.

We ran and ran and at last reached the end of that part of the dunes and there was the back garden of the house we'd been making for.

Once on the snowy lawn, we saw the back of the house in front of us. We crossed the lawn and were planning to go round the house to the front door, when we saw a back door and tried it. It was open. We entered the house and two minutes later we stood in the bedroom of Gerrit's uncle and his wife. They were still fast asleep but woke with a violent start at this sudden intrusion.

"What the hell are you two doing here?" growled Gerrit's uncle.

We explained that we were on the run from a round-up.

The bedroom was at the front of the house and when the uncle jumped out of his bed and looked out of the window he saw German soldiers everywhere.

Hastily, he took us downstairs, opened a secret trap-door in the floor of the sitting-room, and we crawled under the floor. He threw us some blankets and sent his daughter onto the lawn, where she found two sets of prints in the snow, leading from the dunes to the house, one of shoes and the other bare feet. She erased them straightaway and this was a wise precaution, as German soldiers crossed the garden now and then. Whenever this happened Uncle played some music on a gramophone which alerted us that danger was near.

At 2 p.m. the round-up was at last over and Uncle opened the trap-door and called, "You can come out!"

"There is a German standing with a pistol against his head. Stay here," whispered the cautious Gerrit, but everything was OK.

It was only much later that we found out how many incredibly lucky coincidences had blessed our flight that morning.

The Germans had expected many boys to flee into that particular part of the dunes and had posted a lot of armed soldiers everywhere to catch them, which they indeed managed to do. Many were caught.

Somehow we had just run round all those soldiers, turning left when they were to our right and turning right when they were to our left. We had thought all the time that we were quite alone in those dunes, while in reality they had been crawling with soldiers and fleeing young men.

Moreover we had approached the house of Gerrit's uncle from the only direction where the soldiers in front, and at the sides, of the house could not see us.

Finally (but this I found out forty years later when Gerrit and I met after a long time and were reminiscing about the terrible 6 December round-up) that back door should have been locked. If it had been we would have walked around the house straight into the arms of the soldiers. It was open, however, because the housekeeper had come home the previous evening, rather the worse for drink, and had forgotten to lock it.

Close on 3000 men were caught that day and immediately transported to a camp in Rees, just across the German border. It was a very bad camp, offering practically no shelter in that severe winter, and moreover spotted typhus broke out. Many young men died.

I am not one of your strong silent men. With my height of nearly two metres and a rather weak constitution, I would have been one of the first victims.

I sometimes wonder how great the odds were against us on that 6 December, a day that still lives on in Haarlem's collective memory. We swam as fish through a fine-meshed net and did not even realise it. Mathematically speaking, our chances were minimal.

Multiply all the coincidental avoidances of German soldiers with our approach to the house from the only safe direction and with the door that happened to be unlocked and you come up with a statistical impossibility. I was literally saved by a drunken housekeeper.

Exactly 50 years later, on 6 December 1994 at 2 p.m., I received a telephone call from Canada. I picked up the receiver and heard a gruff voice shout, "You can come out!"

"Who is that?" I asked.

My old friend Gerrit, living in Canada, laughed and said, "That is what my uncle cried through the trap-door exactly 50 years ago."

The following year I took a photograph of the back door that had saved our lives, with the friendly consent of the people living there at present, and sent it to Gerrit as a Christmas card.

Coincidences on 6 December 1944 – so many that it is ungrateful to give them that name.

The Famine Winter went from bad to worse. We lived on sugar-beet and tulip bulbs. One thing needed to prepare those foods was imperative – heat. We had to get fuel and the only thing that could be used was wood. So every morning I took my hatchet, sneaked over the road and went to our former neighbour, also evacuated, who had permission to gather kindling in a nearby wood.

Of course that was absolutely insufficient for two hungry families so we sawed whole trees down when no one was looking, and as fast as possible reduced them to kindling.

One day, in February, with an icy-cold wind swirling round me, I went home with my bag of wood balanced on my left shoulder and my hatchet in my right hand. I reached the deserted road (cars were something of a distant memory) and began to cross it, but I had hardly begun when a German soldier appeared, riding a bicycle. He came at me very fast.

All young men my age were always arrested straightaway and the situation looked extremely dangerous. Then, when he was about three yards away from me, we both of us became aware of the same fact: he had forgotten his pistol.

He looked at me and I looked at him and I was absolutely sure that I was going to kill him. I waggled my hatchet a little bit in my right hand, ready to murder him. He saw in my eyes what I was planning. He was rather young, perhaps 18 years old, fair, with an innocent face. He swerved aside and fled from me as fast as his pedals would go.

At that time I hardly gave it a thought, but when I reached maturity I discovered with some horror that inside me, too, there lurked a killer and that I had nearly let it out that day.

That coincidental forgetting of his pistol saved his life and saved me from becoming a killer and perhaps saved lots of other people, because the murder of a German soldier spelled disaster for the neighbourhood where it happened.

What has become of this boy? Then he was the ruthless enemy. Now I wonder about him. Did he survive the war? Become a father and a grandfather? Looking back on that encounter without the feelings of burning hate that possessed us then, I see a rather nice kid. It was one of the most "touch-and-go" situations I have ever been in. There, but for the grace of God, I would have become a murderer.

I will end this chapter on a lighter note.

It was 28 June 1992, my birthday. My wife and I were driving from Montauroux where we had been on holiday, to Avignon where we had to catch the motor-rail which would take us back to Holland, more than 1000 kilometres to the north.

It was a warm Sunday and there was hardly any traffic on the lonely roads we had chosen for the journey to Avignon.

At 12.30 p.m., when we were driving along a road where other traffic seemed to have become extinct, I said: "Let's stop here, sit under the trees over there and have our picnic."

There was a small lay-by, partly covered with high grass, and I slowly backed into it.

Suddenly we heard a bang, a crunching noise, and received a nasty jolt. I put the car into first gear and tried to drive forward but it was stuck.

We got out to investigate the cause of the trouble and discovered that there was a concrete pole, completely hidden in the high grass.

I had nicely speared my car on it and there it was, lodged against the underside, just in front of the right back wheel.

We took all the luggage out and tried to use the jack to get the car dislodged but to no avail. We were hopelessly stuck.

A lady passing us on a bicycle informed us that no help was to be expected from any garage on a Sunday in this region. The nearest inhabited place was a monastery a couple of miles back.

There we were, in the middle of nowhere, and we had to catch our train. I tend to get hopelessly flustered in unexpected situations, but my wife said everything would turn out all right. She had hardly spoken these memorable words, when around the bend on that silent, lonely road, there appeared two bright red cars, the same colour as my own.

They had English number-plates. They stopped and the driver in the front car asked, "What is the matter?"

"I am stuck," I said.

Two men got out and then two women. The men looked strong, in their early 40s, with wiry bodies like those of construction workers. The women were slightly plump and looked rather jolly.

The man who had first spoken to me walked round my car and examined the situation. Then, with a nod, he summoned the other three.

They took up positions behind my car (I ineffectually just beside them) and took hold of the bumper. The leader counted one . . . two . . . three! and, as easily as if it had been a feather, they neatly heaved the car free from its obstruction.

173

All the time we were with those people there was no small talk. They just did their job in an extremely capable and disciplined way, the women no less than the men.

When I thanked them profusely the leader gave me a very odd smile, as if he harboured some secret joke. Then they got into their cars and with a wave of their hands drove away.

Not wanting to stay in that place any longer, we put the luggage back and drove away but, though for miles on end there were no side roads and sometimes we could see a considerable distance ahead, we did not see those two bright red cars again.

It was only later that I thought, "It was exactly like the stories in my book *Meetings With Angels*. And: "Why didn't I talk to them, ask for their address?" Something that had always struck me in the stories people had told me was the absence of small talk. Were they really from England and was their appearance an amazing coincidence, or were they something else? From Angel-land, perhaps? But they were such ordinary people to look at.

And another question: " How great, statistically speaking, was the chance that these two English cars should appear just at the right moment?" We had hardly seen any foreign cars during our stay in France, let alone English ones. It was not yet the season.

There was another hidden coincidence in this story. We were helped at about 12.40 p.m. This was Central European Summer Time. The real time was 11 a.m.

It was my birthday. Exactly 67 years ago on a Sunday morning I was stuck in my mother's womb and at 11 a.m. the gynaecologist with some difficulty had finally managed to deliver me into this world.

We have assembled enough material about coincidences by now to try and answer the question:

WHAT IS COINCIDENCE?

WE MUST NOW try to find an answer to the question.

First let us summarize what we have found thus far:

– Coincidences are always surprising, revealing relationships between events, human beings, things, and natural phenomena that we could never have found out by ourselves.

– Coincidences do not seem to differentiate between the living and non-living, connecting people as easily with each other as with things, or even with forces in nature like lightning.

– Coincidences often speak in symbols and appear in clusters.

– Coincidences are fun-loving animal-friendly, and seem to be at home with numbers and names.

– Coincidences crowd in as soon as people become creative.

– Coincidences love romance.

– Coincidences can definitely be prophetic.

– Coincidences like to help in minor, everyday affairs.

– Coincidences can help in difficult situations and even save lives.

– Coincidences are usually beneficial: but the phenomenon in itself is not tame and when one treats it lightly, it can become quite alarming.

– Coincidences try to evade regimentation (astrology, Tarot) and become elusive when one tries to force them to obey. The phenomenon can become an obsession with some people.

This is quite a bewildering list. It looks as if we have returned to the beginning and found a mystery. Have we found life itself?

Why are we no closer to answering our question: "What is coincidence?"

Yet, long ago, an answer to this question had already been provided.

In Old Testament times the High Priest of Israel on the Day of Atonement had to enter the holy of holies in the temple to stand in the presence of the Lord.

Weinreb has told us that in Jewish tradition something is remembered that is not mentioned in the Bible.

The night preceding this most solemn of all events of the year, the High Priest would be subjected to intensive scrutiny by his fellow priests and they would give him the third degree. They jeered at him, snapped their fingers under his nose and tried to get a confession out of him.

A confession? To what?

They tried to get from him an admission that at some point during the year, he had believed that something in his life had happened just by chance, coincidentally.

Conclusion

what is coincidence?

At last, after a whole night, he would break down in tears and swear to his tormentors that he really had not, even for one brief moment, believed in coincidence. During the whole year that he had been High Priest the thought had not entered his head.

Only then would his fellow priests be satisfied and leave him alone.

Their action was not dictated by some sadistic form of zeal, but by genuine concern for their boss. They knew that if he stood before the Lord with a past in which he – even if it were only for the blink of an eye – had assumed that something in his life had happened by accident, there was a flaw in his character and he might not survive the encounter.

Even then, when he entered the holy of holies, they would tie a golden chain to his ankle in case he might be struck down and die. As no one was allowed to enter the holy of holies except the High Priest, those standing outside could then pull his body out without having entered the forbidden place.

The name "Gouweket" ("Gold Chain") is still borne by certain Jewish families who trace their descent from an ancient High Priest.

Why was it thought to be such a terrible shortcoming in the character of the High Priest to believe in coincidence? A shortcoming grave enough to give him a weak spot in his body, threatening his very life when he stood in that highly-charged atmosphere before the Living Lord?

Because in those times the spiritual authorities still knew that coincidence as pure chance was a fallacy. They were aware of the fact that coincidence was one of the ways in which the Lord could speak to a person.

From time to time people ask me during consultation, "Why is it that men or women say that the Lord has told them something? I never hear His voice."

Of course there are people who hear God's voice and act upon it (and they are wise to do so) but as far as I can evaluate the situation, they belong to a small minority. Most people indeed hear nothing and many people who say that they hear something are caught in an illusion bred by their own desires.

The "small, still voice": Elijah heard so clearly on Horeb (1 Kings 19:12) is silent. Perhaps in our 20th century there is too much noise to hear it.

For those people who long for the small, still voice and yet do not hear anything, the voice of coincidence often speaks loud and clear.

By observing coincidence conscientiously they become aware of the fact that life, though seemingly chaotic at first sight, is not such a haphazard business after all. Through the chaos or drabness or silence one can catch glimpses of beautiful structures. At one point it is only vague, dream-like, at another it is so intense that it translates itself into a feeling of "I am being cared for."

One can often rely on coincidence.

In my profession one patient gives me a piece of information which can be applied directly to the next one. The coincidence is a message in disguise.

A chance meeting, as we have seen, can trigger a whole series of events.

This makes every moment precious because at all times, especially at unexpected times, adventure is just around the corner.

Sometimes one ponders a problem, takes rather absent-mindedly a book from the bookcase, opens it and there on the page lying open is the solution to the problem.

I have also observed that when I clearly formulate a question in my morning prayer, I can, so to speak, wait for a coincidence to give me the right answer.

I learned from that wonderful old evangelist, Corrie ten Boom, an important lesson: "If you need ten pounds, four shillings and six-pence, do not ask for just money or for eleven pounds, but ask for the exact amount you need."

Under the influence of the more abstract ideas about God that are flooding Western society (coming from Eastern religions), we have forgotten that our own civilisation has been built on the foundation of the Bible and in that book God is described not as a distant potentate, or an abstract force, but as a loving father. If that image of Him is true, we are allowed to ask Him for ten pounds, four shillings and sixpence, just as our own children would do when they need exactly that amount of money.

I have already said that forcing coincidence to appear in any other way, such as in astrology, Tarot or *I Ching*, is in my view not relevant any more. It is as if we had thrown out watches away and reverted to sundials.

I am not downgrading the historical value of these methods but I encourage people not to use them, just to pray in a trusting manner. Magic can be fun but we should leave it to great entertainers like Paul Daniels. Nowadays we have a direct approach to God. We had better use that instead of trying the indirect way.

Let us try and answer that difficult question: "What is coinci-dence?"

It now becomes clear that the question cannot be answered because it was wrong.

What I mean is this:–

Imagine that someone asks "Why don't elephants' wings have feathers?"

The question cannot be answered because the question itself is wrong.

So is the question: "WHAT IS COINCIDENCE?"

It can no more be answered than the one about the feathers on elephants' wings. The question should have been:

"WHO IS COINCIDENCE?"

Then the answer stares you in the face straightaway.

Coincidence is one of the subtle and modest ways in which God talks to His children. He wishes for our love, not our fear, and by means of coincidence He gives us little hints of His presence.

Coincidence is God's voice.

What about bad coincidences happening? Are they His voice too?

On the whole I have found that coincidences are usually benevolent.

Yet, sometimes, one seems to stand in the wrong place. A sliding glass door hits your face, or you jump from your bicycle onto an uneven piece of road and sprain your ankle, or – far worse – you say the wrong word in the wrong company.

If the usual benevolent coincidences are the hints God drops to those who are beginning to wonder about Him, the occasional bad coincidences need not be negative in their effects for those who know Him slightly better. Afterwards they can often see that it is a blessing in disguise, confirming what Paul said to the Romans: "And we know that all things work together for good to them that love God" (Romans 8:28).

The accident may slow you down at the right moment; saying the wrong thing can teach you the power hidden in words.

But I do not want to dwell on the occasional slightly darker side of coincidence.

This is a book about joy, not grief.

It is about the overwhelming joy just waiting around the corner until you call for it.

As a lover of detective stories, of course I knew from the beginning "whodunnit". I knew what the answer to the question would be, for there is a very old piece of wisdom which says that in our life we should proceed from the initial question, "*What* is this?" (posed by all children when they begin to talk) to, "*Who* is this?"

Our whole path of life should be a walk from *What* to *Who*.

A voyage from an encounter with the world around us towards a meeting with Him who created that world.

Coincidences can be signposts along that road.

As a conclusion to all these adventures let us end with a poem. It can be considered as an "Ode to coincidence". It was the favourite poem of Corrie ten Boom.

"My life is but a weaving, between my God and me.
I do not choose the colours, He worketh steadily.
Ofttimes he weaves sorrow, and I in foolish pride,
Forget He sees the upper, and I the underside.
Not till the loom is silent and shuttles cease to fly
Will God unroll the canvas and explain the reason why.
The dark threads are as needful in the skilful weaver's hand
As the threads of gold and silver in the pattern He has planned."

God bless you.

Barnes, B. O., *Hypothyroidism, One Unsuspected Illness*. Harper & Row. 1976. ISBN o 69001029 X.

Baschwitz, K., *Heksen on Heksenprocessen*. Arbeiderspers. 1964.

Begich, Dr N. (and Jeanne Manning), *Angels Don't Play This HAARP*. Earthpulse Press, ISBN 09648812 o 9.

Behe, Michael J., *Darwin's Black Box*. The Free Press. ISBN 0684827549.

BIBLES: *The Companion Bible, 198 Appendices by Bullinger. Concordant Version, The Sacred Scriptures*. Concordant Publishing Concern. 2823 East Sixth Street, Los Angeles, 23 California, USA.

ten Boom, Corrie, *The Hiding-Place*. H. Revell Company. New Jersey.

Bullinger, E. W., *The Witness of the Stars*. Lamp Press (nowadays USA edition).
Number in Scripture: Its Supernatural Design and Spiritual Significance. 1895.

Chaitow, Leon, *Vaccination and Immunisation*. The C. W. Daniel Company. ISBN 085207 191 4.

Carroll, Lewis, *The Complete Illustrated Works*. Chancellor Press. ISBN o 907486215.

Colborn (Dumanoski and Myers), *Our Stolen Future*. Dutton. ISBN o 525 93982 2.

Dante, *The Divine Comedy* (translated by Dorothy L. Sayers). Penguin Books.

Denton, Michael, *Evolution: A Theory in Crisis*. Adler & Adler. ISBN o 917561 05 8.

Fluoride, Journal of the International Society for Fluoride Research.
Volume 29, No. 4, p. 190. L. B. Zhao c.s. "Effect of a High Fluoride Water Supply on Children's Intelligence".
Volume 30, No. 2. Prof. Schatz. "Paradoxical Effects: Critique of a Study".

Gleick, James, *Chaos*. Penguin Books. ISBN o 140092501.

Goldhagen, D. J., *Hitler's Willing Executioners*. Abacus. ISBN o 349 10786 6.

de Graaff, B., *Spion in de Tuin*. Sdu. ISBN 90 12 08005 3.

Grant, Dr E., *The Bitter Pill*. Elm Tree Books. London. ISBN 90215147 9 6.
Sexual Chemistry. Cedar. Mandarin Paperback. ISBN o 7493 1363 3.

Halevi, Z. b S., *Tree of Life*. Rider & Company. ISBN 009 112261 9.

Hildebrand, *De Camera Obscura*. Bohn. 1940.

Jung, C. J., *I Ching*. Amsterdam. Translation Richard Wilhelm.

Janduz, *Les 360 Degrés du Zodiaque: Symbolisés par l'Image et par la Cabale*. Niclaus. 1939.

Jones, E. J. & Gladstone, J. F., *The Red King's Dream, of Lewis Carroll In Wonderland*. Jonathan Cape. ISBN o 224 04020 0.

Kolisko, L., *Physiologischer und physikalischer Nachweis der Wirksamkeit kleinster Entitäten*. Arbeitsgemeinschaft Antropos. Artzte 1923–1959.

Koppejan, Helene & Wim, *Beeldgids van de Dierenriem I, II, III*. Ankh Hermes. ISBN 90 202 16708.

Kübler Ross, Elisabeth, *Over de dood en het leven daarna*. Ambo. ISBN 90 263
    0716 0.

Kushner, H. S., *When Bad Things Happen to Good People*. Schocken Books,
    New York. 1981.

Lewis, C. S., *That Hideous Strength*. Pan Books. 1955.

The Four Loves. Fount Paperbacks. ISBN 0 00 620799 5.

Milne, A. A., *Winnie-the-Pooh*. Leipzig. Bernhard Tauchnitz. 1939.

Moolenburgh, H. C., *Fluoride, the Fight for Freedom*. Mainstream. ISBN
    1 85158 040 9.

Meetings with Angels. The C. W. Daniel Company. ISBN 0 85207 260 0.

A Handbook of Angels. The C. W. Daniel Company. ISBN 0 85207 169 8.

De Wetenschap Kent Geen Tranen. Ankh Hermes. ISBN 90 202 4906 1.

Beschavingsziekten en Gezondheid. Ankh Hermes. ISBN 90 202 0707 7.

Morel, Franz, *BEV-Fibel*. 1983. SIBEV.

Morris, Henry, *The Long War Against God*. Baker Book House Co. ISBN
    08010 6257 8.

The Genesis Record. Baker Book House Co. ISBN 0 8010 6004 4.

Men of Science, Men of God. Master Books, ISBN 08905l 080 6.

The Genesis Flood. Presbyteries and Reformed Publ. ISBN 0 87552 338 2.

Naeff, *School idyllen*.

Nexus, June/July 1997. The Gatto Article.

Nicoll, Maurice, *Psychological Commentaries on the Teachings of G. I.
    Gurdjieff and P. D. Ouspensky*. Vincent Stuart '57.

Nieuwe, Golflengte, *Psychopolotiek*.

Ouspensky, P. D., *A New Model of the Universe* (Dutch Edition Servire).

Perkins, Ch. E., *The Truth About Water Fluoridation*.

The Fluoridation Educational Society.

Playfair, G. L., *If This Be Magic*. J. Cape. ISBN 0 224 023381.

Raum & Zeit, Ehlers Verlag. No. 80, 81, 82, 83, 84, 85.

Rudhyar, Dane, *The Astrology of Personality*. Dutch Edition Astrologie,
    Aanleg en Karakter De Friehoek. 1950.

Scholz, W. von, *De rol van toeval en noodlot in ons leven*. Elsevier. 1960.

Schwenk, Theodor, *Das Sensibele Chaos*. Freier Geistesleben. 1963.

Scott Peck, M., *People of the Lie: The Hope for Healing Human Evil*.
    Touchstone Books. New York. ISBN 0 671 52816 5.

Shalev, Meir, *De Bijbel*. Nu. Vassaluci. ISBN 90 5000 0045.

Sheldrake, Rupert, *A New Science of Life: The Hypothesis of Formative
    Causation*. Butler & Tanner. 1981. ISBN 0 85634 1150.

with Matthew Fox, *Natural Grace: Dialogues on Science & Spirituality*.
    Bloomsbury. ISBN 0 7475 2627 3.

Simonton, Carl O., (with Stephanie Simonton and James Creighton),
    Getting Well Again. Tarcher Inc. ISBN 087477 070 X.

Slate, B. Ann & Alan Berry, *Big Foot*. Bantam Books. ISBN 0553 02968 1.

Smits, Tinus, *Het Post-vaccinaal syndroom smits-voorhoeve*. ISBN 90 003326
    15.

Natuurwetpartij, *Genetische Manipulatie*. Fact Sheet on Genetic Manipulation of Soya and Maize.

Sträuli, Robert, *Origenes der Diamantene*. ABZ Verlag. ISBN 3855160058.

Swedenborg, Emanuel, *Arcana Caelesta* (translated by John Eliot). The Swedenborg Society. London. ISBN 0 85448 089 7.

Tailleur, Max, *Geloof me. Becht*. Amsterdam. ISBN 90 230 0161 3.

Talbot, Michael, *The Holographic Universe*. Harper Perennial. ISBN 0 06 092258 3.

Tiemens, Willem, *Facetten van de slag in Arnhem*. De Gooise Uitgeverij. ISBN 90 269 4570 1.

van Tijn, Maartje, *Midraggim II*.

Verheyen, Ing. J. T., *Genezend Water*. Keerbergen.

Waite, A. E., *The Pictorial Key to the Tarot*. University Books. 1959.

Weinreb, F., Courses 1964–1970.

De Bijbel Als Schepping. Servire. 1963.

Ik die verborgen ben (Esther). Servire. 1967.

Das Buch Jona. Origo. 1970.

Die Langen Schatten des Krieges. Thauros Verlag. ISBN 3 88411 0357.

Wurmbrand, Dr Richard, *The Underground Church*.

Tortured for Christ.

Yiamouyiannis, J., *Fluoride: The Aging Factor*. Health Action Press. ISBN 0913571 008.

Index